Issues in Quality Child Care

Issues in Quality Child Care
A Boys Town Perspective

Contributors
Val J. Peter, JCD, STD
David D. Coughlin, Ph.D.
Daniel L. Daly, Ph.D.
Robert E. Larzelere, Ph.D.
Mark Jones, Ph.D.
Andrea Criste, M.Ed.
Thomas R. Criste, M.H.D.
Jeff Tierney, M.Ed.
Kay Graham, M.H.D.
Carolyn Novicoff, M.S.
Paula Jones
Robert Pick, M.S.
Clark J. Toner, J.D.

Editors
Tom Dowd, M.A.
Michael N. Sterba, M.H.D.
Terry Hyland
Ron Herron

BOYS
TOWN
PRESS

Book Credits

Production: Christine Grantski
Layout: Michael Bourg
Cover Design: Brian Wilson

Issues in Quality Child Care

Published by The Boys Town Press
Father Flanagan's Boys' Home
Boys Town, Nebraska 68010

Publisher's Cataloging in Publication
(Prepared by Quality Books Inc.)

Issues in quality child care: a Boys Town perspective/
    contributors Val J. Peter... [et al.]; editors Tom Dowd
    ... [et al.]. – 1st ed.
      p. cm.
      Includes index.
      ISBN: 1-889322-17-2

      1. Discipline of children 2. Child psychology. 3.
Behavior therapy for children. I. Peter, Val J. II.
Father Flanagan's Boys' Home.

HQ770.4.I77 1998   649'.64
                                 QBI98-115

10   9   8   7   6   5   4   3   2   1

Table of Contents

Introduction

For more than 80 years, Boys Town's mission has been to change the way America cares for her at-risk children. In an environment of genuine caring, we have established proven child-care technologies to teach children how to overcome their problems and change their lives for the better. Competence and compassion are the hallmarks of this mission, which continues to grow every day.

This collection of articles describes how Boys Town carries out its mission. Since its humble beginnings, the Home's caretakers have had the foresight to develop systems of care that meet the ever-changing needs of troubled children. Our research is constantly going forward to address the most difficult behavioral problems of youth. Each year we learn more and apply it so that more kids can get better.

    The Boys Town Teaching Model, the focus of this book, is the result of that research and years of experience working with troubled and at-risk children. The Model has proven successful in diverse settings and situations with a variety of youth populations. Replicated at Boys Town sites across the country, and in a variety of child-care programs and school systems, it is a practical approach to helping children learn how to replace negative behaviors with positive behaviors.

    The essence of the Boys Town Teaching Model is building relationships and teaching skills. These two components are dependent on each other and work simultaneously. In order to describe how these components originated and developed, the first article of the book presents the history and growth of the Model. Then we look at humane ways to build and strengthen relationships with children. These methods are described in "The Vital Signs of Relationships for Caregivers." The next three articles explain the methods caregivers use in teaching skills. "Quality Teaching" focuses on correcting inappropriate behavior and providing children with positive alternatives. "Why Do Kids Misbehave?"

discusses the causes of inappropriate behavior in children. "Crisis Teaching" explains a process for dealing with more serious misbehavior that teaches children how to maintain self-control in situations where they would otherwise become angry or upset. The final article, "Reducing Aggression in Children," addresses a pervasive problem in our society and provides practical strategies that can help young people control their aggressive behavior.

Many young people today no longer have control over their lives. They are being controlled by their environments, peers, drugs, alcohol, anger, hostility, or hopelessness. Their problem behaviors are a direct result of what or who controls them. Since caregivers have to compete with all of these negative influences, youth must be offered something that they believe is better. What the Boys Town Teaching Model offers is "empowerment."

Gradually, the kids learn how to make good decisions on their own, how to be responsible for their behaviors, how to appropriately solve problems, and how to change from being a person who is controlled to a person who is in control. They gain trust in God and confidence in themselves, and their self-esteem grows.

In order for caregivers to teach life skills youth need for success, accurate understanding and skillful implementation of the techniques described in these articles are essential. We hope this book can help you in that process, and we applaud your efforts to improve the lives of the children in your care.

Developmental History of the Boys Town Teaching Model

By Fr. Val J. Peter

To understand the concept of helping children learn new behaviors, one must first realize that we are in the "business" of bringing healing and hope to children and families. Everything we do is rooted in the human experience – the successes, the failures, the progress, the obstacles. Children are human beings, not products on an assembly line. And we at Boys Town are caregivers, not robots programmed to perform the same task, the same way, every day. It is true that technology and theory are necessary, but so is genuine compassion and concern. Technology without compassion is pure manipulation. And love and compassion without good science is pure sentimentality.

Ours is a noble cause – to help children gain the knowledge, skills, and ability to make wise decisions that will enable them to find success in their lives. Achieving those lofty goals requires dedicated people armed with extraordinary tools. That's where the history of the Boys Town Teaching Model begins.

While the Boys Town Teaching Model has its basis in learning theory, it has not adopted a "mechanistic" view of how a child learns, as have other models that take this approach. In the Boys Town Model, the child is an active participant in the teaching and learning that occurs. The child isn't merely told how to behave; he or she learns positive behaviors and how to choose to use them in many different situations. This "empowerment," or self-help, approach combines the active participation of the child with the active teaching of the parent or caretaker. The strength of this approach is that it teaches children prosocial skills and helps them build healthy relationships with others.

The goal of this approach is not to control children, except at the start when they must learn the rules and guidelines. The goal is to help children take control of their own lives. By learning self-help skills, children can change the way they think, feel, and act. This is a learning process. Boys

Town's teaching methods utilize behavioral principles, while allowing children to integrate their thoughts and feelings into this learning process. And, unlike many other learning theory models, Boys Town uses external reinforcement, where appropriate, to promote and maintain skill-learning and relationship development. This allows children to change intrinsically. Inadequate thought patterns change, negative feelings diminish, and inappropriate behaviors are replaced by positive behaviors for the youth and others.

Over the years, the Boys Town Model has not remained static or fixed; rather, it is constantly changing. This means that we regularly incorporate what we are learning from our clinical work with children or from research that reveals new information about the problems children face and how to address them. But while our Model is open to change, some things remain permanent: our solid behavioral base, our emphasis on internalization and generalization, our spiritual and moral foundations, and our reliance on research and clinical learning.

In order to better understand this progression, it is beneficial to look back on the "life" of our Model and compare its development to that of a child.

When raising very small children, moms and dads rightly place tight restrictions on their environments and set limits as to where they can and cannot go. ("Don't go out of the yard." "Don't cross the street.") We do the same thing at Boys Town when a child first comes to us. The rules that create a carefully structured environment may make it appear that we are rigid, but we set these tight boundaries to help the healing process so the child can learn self-control. Our children's ability to reason isn't very good when they come to us. It is our responsibility to help them.

When the Boys Town Model was "born" in 1975, we took this basic approach. The Model had its origins in a research project called Achievement Place, conducted at the University of Kansas in the late 1960s and early 1970s. Boys Town adopted this work, expanded it, enlarged it, and developed it more fully.

Like good parents, we were protective of our new approach and its boundaries, and set very clear expectations and limits. Some may have regarded these as too strict, not realizing that in the early stages of development they were necessary to ensure continuation and progress of the Model. Since it was so new, it was important to strictly adhere to its components and apply it "by the book." Those early days were a time of cautious, steady growth for the Model. And just as parents must act to protect their children, Boys Town acted to safeguard the clear successes we were having with children.

At the same time, Boys Town remained open to change. As the Model grew – just as a child grows – we developed, incorporated and generated new ideas, learned from our experiences, and began to find new ways to help children. This explains how the Model can have permanent elements, which ensure that caregivers continue to use it as it was meant to be used, and still experience change, which encourages program development and improvement to help children and families.

It is important here to remember how our mission of caring for children started. Boys Town began taking in needy and troubled children in 1917, when Father Edward Flanagan founded his home for boys in Omaha, Nebraska. In those early days, Father Flanagan established three basic principles for the type of care he would provide for the youngsters. These three are what we would call his "program," or "child–care technology."

First, he believed that boys should be rehabilitated, not incarcerated. The rehabilitation he was talking about was creating a family of boys whom society had given up on. Father Flanagan passionately believed in freedom, equality, and justice, and welcomed boys of all races and creeds to live and learn in the Boys Town family.

Second, Father Flanagan believed that youngsters also could be rehabilitated through education, which started with the three R's – reading, 'riting, and 'rithmetic. This education continued as boys learned a vocation or trade, something that would enable them to make a successful living. Father Flanagan knew that if kids wanted to be productive members of society, they needed someone to teach them the necessary vocational skills – shoemaking, barbering, carpentry, printing, etc. – at an early age.

Third, Father Flanagan believed that young people, if they received the proper guidance, could learn self-government. The youth elected their own mayor, councilmen, and other officers, and everyone had an active voice in the Home's operation. In today's parlance, we could call this "empowerment."

The shared emphasis on these three areas made up the child-care science of Boys Town in the early days. But that was only half of the genius of

Father Flanagan. Boys Town not only had a head (the science) but also a big heart. Yes, the other half of the genius of Boys Town was the heart: the love for children and the passion and compassion to bring hope and healing.

From 1917 on, this approach benefited thousands of young people who were able to change their lives for the better at Boys Town. But in the late 1960s and early 1970s, youngsters began to come to Boys Town with new problems – physical, emotional, and sexual abuse, drug and alcohol use, suicide, and violence of all sorts – that our old child-care science could not "fix." Yes, we still had enormous love for the children, but love alone could not bring hope and healing. Our heart was still there. What we needed was a new approach, a new set of child-care technologies for a new generation of children. Remember: The heart without the head is pure sentimentality, just as the head without the heart is pure manipulation. It was out of this need that the Boys Town Teaching Model was created.

The Model grew and prospered in the 1970s and early 1980s. So successful did it become that two kinds of expansion were called for: first, geographic expansion, and second, technological transfer to new programs.

So, in 1985, monumental changes occurred as Boys Town began a national expansion effort. There were two big questions to be answered when the program moved into various parts of the country: How would the Model work in different geographical settings? Could the Model be replicated? We began to see these questions answered with positive results as we established Boys Town programs and sites in major metropolitan areas.

Then, in 1988, we expanded the Model to include four new service areas: parent training, in-home services, emergency shelter services, and treatment foster care. In 1990, training programs were added, including educational training and hospital services. We discovered that the technology could be transferred effectively from one program to another.

The combination of our nationwide expansion and the creation of new programs flooded the Model with a wealth of new information, new ideas, and new technology. This resulted in more change and set the stage for another cycle of evolution within the Model, beginning in 1996.

Learning how to do things better requires being open to change. But our desire to change has not meant abandoning the basic principles and ideas that have made our Model so effective and so attractive. As we have developed new ways of teaching kids, training caregivers, and promoting programs, we simply built (and continue to build) on the behavioral base of what we know works best for children and families.

Earlier, we compared the development of the Boys Town Model to that of a child. A child is constantly growing – physically, emotionally, and intellectually. This child's world is different from what it was when he was a toddler. There are new things to experience and new ways to interact with the people in his life. Yet almost everything this child does is firmly rooted in the lessons he learned and the experiences he had earlier in life. He retains and remembers the basic rules and boundaries, and builds upon them as he develops and grows.

When Father Flanagan founded his Home for orphaned and wayward boys in 1917, he knew they would respond to kindness, compassion, and discipline. They did. More than 80 years later, even with the mind-boggling array of problems our youth face, these are still the qualities that help young boys and girls turn their lives around.

As we said earlier, the major constants of the Boys Town Model are teaching skills and

13

building relationships. Teaching skills is what helps kids learn new ways of thinking, new ways of feeling good, and new ways of behaving. By teaching, we give kids the skills they need in order to take control of their lives and be successful. Whether it's a parent who wants to teach his daughter the skill of problem-solving, or a staff member in a youth shelter trying to help a youth learn anger-control strategies, teaching is the key.

At the same time, helping children build relationships enables them to feel better about themselves and their lives and to feel more hopeful for the future. In addition, a strong relationship creates a bond of trust between a caregiver and a youth. A child is much more likely to learn from, and try to imitate, an adult who is warm, fun to be with, sincere, and caring. Many of the kids who come to Boys Town have been in hurtful relationships. They have learned to be mistrustful, and have a hard time getting along with others. Reaching out to a child and helping remove the layers of distrust and anger that have built up over time is one of the most difficult and, at the same time, promising tasks there is. But once a child responds, and realizes that someone has his or her best interests at heart, progress is swift and the rewards are great for both the youth and the caregiver.

The spirit of both continuity and change have brought Boys Town to where it is today. We realize that just as there will always be children and families who need help, there will always be better ways to help them. And while the Boys Town Teaching Model was built on the lessons of the past, it needs always to keep its sights set firmly on the future as well.

"The work will continue, you see, whether I am there or not, because it is God's work, not mine."

– Father Edward Flanagan

The Vital Signs
of Relationships
for Caregivers

"She was a source of inspiration for me. She's the first one who thought I could make something of myself."

— Angie, age 16

"He was the only one who encouraged me to do better. Thanks to him, I not only got my diploma; I got a real lesson about how to enjoy the world around me."

— Reggie, age 19

"She never gave up on me. When I wanted to quit, she would say I couldn't, and then find some way to convince me that I really could succeed. She created the confidence I have now because I certainly didn't have it before I met her."

— Miranda, age 20

> *"My teacher is the best teacher ever. She makes me feel good even when I'm tired or sad."*
>
> – Pernell, age 8

These testimonials illustrate the tremendous impact that caring adults have on the young people with whom they work. And these certainly are not isolated cases. Many of us can remember someone outside of our family who recognized our hidden potential and gave us the skills we needed to grow and develop. They pointed us in the right direction and helped us succeed.

People who work directly with youth have a great influence on their lives. Regardless of what capacity you serve in – teacher, minister, day-care provider, counselor, coach, youth group leader, or just someone who likes to help kids – young people rely on you for the guidance and nurturance necessary to make their lives better. Certainly, the kind of help these children need varies a great deal. Some may need a small nudge in the right direction; others require much, much more. Some of these young people desperately need an adult to respect and admire. Many are hurt, abused, angry, and vulnerable to the harshness of the world. You are part of the solution in helping them make some sense of it all and move on with their lives.

As our society becomes more diverse, many young people have problems fitting into the mainstream, whether it be the job market, school, or simply getting along with others. The problems of violence, drug and alcohol use and abuse, and other social ills have skyrocketed. The pressure on today's kids is tremendous, and many of them don't have the coping skills necessary to be successful. Tragically, some kids have no one to turn to for help. Amid all of these disruptive and negative influences, however, people like you continue to make positive differences in children's lives. At times, you may even be called on to be a parental substitute and provide a safe and secure environment for the children in your care.

Whether your job description says it or not, if you work with kids, you are a teacher. You teach and model many skills each time you are with a young person. And it's likely that your success relies as much on how you teach as what you teach.

The quality of the relationships you have with your kids is crucial to what they learn. Anyone who works with kids is more successful when he or she combines nurturing with teaching instead of being mechanical and detached. This chapter focuses on what you can do to promote and nourish healthy relationships with your kids.

To some people, this may conjure up images of being "buddies" with the kids, speaking the current slang, or "hanging out" with them. But that's not what we mean by positive relationships. Building healthy, caring relationships goes hand in hand with providing guidance, discipline, and competent instruction. Teaching skills and building relationships are the cornerstones of true education. They are not enemies, and they do not occur in a vacuum. They go together, and they are simultaneous events. When the proper balance is achieved, the results are confident, likable, and successful young people.

Of course, striking a balance between teaching and building relationships is the ideal. Relying too much on building relationships, and ignoring teaching and discipline, will not help young people learn valuable life skills. The opposite also is true. Concentrating on one without using the other is like trying to play on a teeter-totter by yourself; it is unbalanced. Caregivers who are most helpful and successful with children blend warmth and compassion with their teaching, and as skills are learned, relationships grow as well.

Teaching skills and building relationships also are woven into the fabric of everyday life and its wide-ranging events. There will be times of tragedy, sadness, enlightenment, problems, fun, and boredom in all of our lives. Although you may understand that life is not always going to go the way you want, many young people don't yet realize this. Therefore, it is your responsibility (and privilege) to teach your kids as much as you can about what they can do in these situations. Your goal, of course, is to help your kids be the best they can be in many areas of their lives – social, academic, and moral. This is a sizable task by any stretch of the imagination. But it can be done, and when it happens, you will have received one of the greatest rewards in life.

All children are different, each with personal likes and dislikes, opinions, and preferences. Something that works with one child may not work with another. Some kids will learn more quickly than others. But through all of your teaching, it is important that kids realize that we all can learn from one another. They also must realize that even though you may individualize your teaching techniques, you are treating each one of them fairly and have their best interests at heart. You can help them broaden their view of life and teach them that we can live together in friendliness and acceptance. Learning cultural awareness, being sensitive to the rights of others, and respecting other people's differences are valuable lessons for our young people to learn. When you teach these ideals, you empower your kids to use what they have learned in other settings as well.

Let's look more closely at some of the vital signs of relationships, the elements that make a relationship vibrant and worthwhile. You probably possess many of these qualities now. If so, maybe you'll find ways to enhance what you already do. Maybe thinking about these qualities will help you discover new ways to use your relationship potential. Take some time to select a few skills you can learn, and make this part of your goal for personal improvement. Let's face it; if all of us don't continually strive for improvement, the stresses of life tend to push us back into old habits. Then negative behaviors can surface out of our frustration.

The Qualities of Healthy Relationships

It is a good bet that making the following qualities part of your personality will help you maintain happy and healthy relationships with everyone. They will be especially useful as you teach your kids to live happier, richer lives.

Smiling

If you see someone without a smile,
give him one of yours.

Of all of the qualities that show warmth, smiling might be the most important. Meeting or talking with someone who is smiling makes us feel good; it's an invitation to friendship, a sign that a person is approachable and welcomes our presence.

Smiling costs nothing, and yet it is one of the richest gifts we can give others. It makes people feel good inside, comforts people when they are down, and consoles them when they are feeling lonely. Smiling is, or should be, a natural gesture of friendship and good will.

Of course, smiling at the wrong time can be misinterpreted by young people. It is possible that children or teens may think that you're making fun of them, or that you have "something up your sleeve." They may be suspicious or cautious. The cure for that is consistency. If you consistently smile at appropriate times and in appropriate situations, young people will trust you and look forward to seeing you. For the most part, smiling is a key to being viewed as open, easy to talk to, and friendly.

If you frequently are told that you look too serious, then make it a point to smile more. Although it sounds simple, it may be harder than you think. Begin by making it a common practice to greet your kids with a smile the first time you see them each day.

The world is like a mirror; frown at it and it frowns at you; smile, and it smiles too.

Having Fun

Laughter is a tranquilizer that has no side effects.

It's difficult for some adults to have fun with their kids. They might be too worried about losing their authority and control, or afraid that the kids will laugh at them (not with them). Some care-givers may feel that their job is too serious to "trivialize" it by having fun, or that there are so many problems to attend to that they don't have the time. Still others may simply be afraid to show their "human" side because they don't want to appear vulnerable. That's unfortunate. Having fun together is a huge factor in healthy relationships. You don't have to become a party animal and wear lampshades on your head to have fun with kids. There are many healthy ways to allow them to enjoy you and your teaching without losing any respect or authority. In fact, you will most likely create an environment of warmth and acceptance. Let's look at some ways of having fun:

Play

There's a little kid in all of us, but some adults won't let that little kid out to play. Playing is serious stuff; it teaches valuable lessons about life. Sharing, respecting others, taking responsibility, following rules, accepting defeat, and being gracious in victory are some of these lessons that can be taught in a playful environment. The child who has not learned how to play is missing out on one of life's greatest treasures.

Many successful caregivers set some time aside each day for a trivia quiz, a board or word game, playing catch or shooting baskets, or some other enjoyable activity. One teacher we worked with divided her class into teams and had them come up with questions to ask each other on the subject they were studying. After the students handed in the questions, she assigned point values to each one based on its difficulty. Then each Friday, she had a contest where students answered the questions to earn points. Occasionally, she even videotaped the class. It was a novel and exciting way to teach the class material, have fun, and help students build relationships with one another.

Even routine activities can be fun. For example, one caregiver taught his kids how to play a game called "Zits" when they were driving in the van on outings or trips to the store. In this game, everyone decides on a make of car, such as a Volkswagen. Each time one is spotted, the first person who sees it and says "Zits" gets points. Different point values are given for each style: one point for a Rabbit, two points for a "Bug," five points for a bus, and so on. The first one to 21 points wins. And the car must be running; no driving by a car dealership for cheap points. Anyone who mistakenly says "Zits" for a car that isn't a Volkswagen loses points. The kids love it! The game makes even a long drive an enjoyable event.

Humor

If you can laugh at it, you can live with it.

Some people are described as having a "good sense of humor." While the phrase may mean different things to different people, basically it means that a person has the ability to see or perceive the laughable, amusing, and funny events in our lives. Our world is full of comical moments, but, unfortunately, some people are so caught up in other things that they just don't see them.

The ability to laugh and see humor in everyday situations makes other people happy, too. If people often tell you that you're too serious, it's time to lighten up. Dealing with kids is a tough business that's full of ups and downs. If you don't learn how to find humor in what happens, you will constantly dwell on all the bad things. A good sense of humor can insulate you from negative feelings that can get the best of you.

If you don't think you have a sense of humor, you can develop one. And it doesn't have to mean becoming a stand-up comedian. Instead, you can find humor in the media and other resources around you. Look for comical stories. There are plenty of books, tapes, and movies that are genuinely funny. Collect funny stories, comic strips, or cartoons, and give them to your kids. Sometimes, kids won't understand these materials, so you may have to explain what makes them funny. Have fun with puns; there are some real groaners that you can come up with. The main thing is that you show kids how to find some humor in life. They need to know how healthy it is to laugh. Kids need a break from their stresses just as much as adults do.

Learn to Laugh at Yourself

Life is about 10% how you make it,
and 90% how you take it.

27

We all have shortcomings, and we all make mistakes. Any person who can laugh at his or her faults is providing a positive model for young people. If you ever feel like poking fun at someone's mistakes, poke fun at your own.

You must have courage to be able to laugh at yourself. It is easy to blame someone else when things go wrong, but it makes no difference in the long run. Learn to admit your mistakes. Laugh at dumb things you have done. This is not being self-defeating; that only happens when you dwell on your mistakes and do nothing to change them. Laughing at yourself means admitting that you have weaknesses just like other human beings. The difference is that you do it in a funny but truthful manner.

Joking and Teasing (appropriately)

Everyone likes a good joke. Even silly (not tasteless) jokes can bring a few chuckles. But joking and teasing have to be done in a playful, accepting manner, never in ways that seem sarcastic or condescending. A person must be very good at knowing what can and can't be said in certain situations and with certain people. When you're working with kids, it's especially wise to take your time in this area. Test the waters. See if kids understand the purpose and intent of your joking and teasing. If you can make kids laugh without making them feel bad or hurting someone's feelings, you will create a warm and relaxing environment.

Buy a joke book. Learn to tell funny stories, or talk about "silly" things that happened to you when you were growing up. Tell your kids about the "good old days" and how everything has changed. Joke about your generation or the ideas you had way back when. It's nice to look on the bright side of things and have a good laugh once in a while.

It is very important to know how to tease. Never use a mocking or harsh voice. And never say things that could be viewed as disrespectful to a person's race, religion, or personal beliefs. Teasing is appropriate only when kids will perceive it as gentle ribbing; then it is not picking on or bullying someone. Appropriate teasing is a way of showing that you care about someone, not a way to make that person feel bad, which is the goal of cruel teasing.

Teasing usually works best after you have developed a fairly sound relationship with your youth. For example, one teacher had a student named Kevin who was much smaller than the other kids in the class. (He simply was a "late bloomer" and eventually caught up to the others.) One day, one of the other boys was trying to open a bottle of glue to clean out the tip, but just couldn't get the top to budge. Kevin tried and unscrewed the top the first time! From then on, Kevin was good-naturedly called "Hulk" by the rest of the class. Every time the kids called him by his nickname, he'd laugh, flex his muscles, and let out a grunt like a weight-lifter. The teasing was done in a tasteful and caring way. Kevin knew the others weren't making fun of him, and the attention made him feel special.

Nicknames are great ways to give recognition and show fondness for kids. One Little League coach gave each of his players special "tags." He had "Gabe the Babe," "Nate, Skate and Donate," "Buster," "Yogi," "Gentle Ben," and "Greg the Peg." The kids felt a sense of identity and belonging. In fact, the names stuck so well that the boys thought it was odd when someone called them by their real names.

Exaggeration and understatements also are forms of teasing and joking: "He must have eaten a bazillion tacos"; "I don't have the brains God gave a crowbar"; "I'm so broke, I can't pay attention"; "Mom makes biscuits so good that if you put one on your forehead, your tongue would slap you silly." Many situations can be put into a humorous light by using exaggeration or understatement.

Don't underestimate the value of a good sense of humor. Working with kids is difficult; we all know that. There are some serious issues that must be attended to, but not everything is a matter of life and death. Humor provides relief from the everyday stress of life and allows us to relax and enjoy one another's company.

The time to be happy is now; the place
to be happy is here; the way to be happy
is to make others so.

Empathy

There is no better exercise for the heart than
reaching down and lifting someone up.

Empathy means trying to understand another person's situation and feelings. For many people, this is not easy or natural. Many of us grew up being told what we should do and how we should feel. In fact, many of us may even have been taught to deny our true feelings. We heard statements like, "You really don't mean that"; "Shake it off. It's no big deal"; or "There's no reason to feel that way. Straighten up and fly right." Although these statements may be appropriate occasionally, they don't have much effect on changing a child's behavior. And often, the harder you try to convince children that they really aren't feeling what they say they're

31

feeling, the more those feelings seem to stick with them. Kids go through many changes, and often they don't know how to handle new experiences and the emotions that these changes bring. Sometimes, they may feel trapped by their feelings and think that any attempt to change is futile. A kind and caring adult can begin the process of hope and healing. Kids need to learn that negative emotions are a transient part of life and that things will get better. You can teach them that it's okay to feel bad; more importantly, you can help them find the strength in themselves to carry on.

We all know that it's easy to talk to a young person when he or she is happy and has a positive outlook. Dealing constructively with a youth's negative feelings requires much more skill. Using empathy involves identifying with what a person is going through. One thing that helps is to think back to the way you felt in similar situations. Empathy requires you to look at the world through the youth's eyes.

Many children also face the problem of not having a trusted adult they can talk to. Caregivers often have to fill this void by being there when a child needs someone. Today's children face more pressure and experience it sooner than prior generations. Many are forced to grow up too fast.

Furthermore, a larger proportion of children than ever before come from dysfunctional or abusive backgrounds where they were deprived of the love and discipline they need. Although many parents may mean well, some of the children you work with are suffering and need someone with whom they can share their fears and pain. Teachers, counselors, clergy, and other caregivers must accept the responsibility of providing a helping hand and an attentive ear to these children. All kids deserve to reap the benefits of having a caring adult who will listen and acknowledge their feelings.

Some people are perceptive enough to know when it is appropriate to give an empathic response to another person. They may say things like, "It looks like you're angry," or "It looks like you're having a hard time." But those statements lose their impact if they are not said sincerely and compassionately. Merely recognizing the plight of another person isn't enough; you have to understand that what the person is feeling has affected him or her in some way. In other words, you must be willing to "walk a mile in another person's shoes."

Being empathic also does not mean that you fail to give consequences for negative behavior. There's no doubt that the way a person feels affects his or her behavior. However, feelings are not an excuse for misbehavior. Kids need to understand that just because a guy is angry at his boss, he does not have the green light to punch the boss in the nose. Empathy does not replace teaching and consequences; it is simply an important relationship skill that smoothes the way for effective teaching.

Some adults rush to solve a child's problem. They feel that having all of the answers is their primary role. But while giving advice and instructions is very important, there are times when it's best just to listen and understand. Be patient; there will be time to solve the problems later. Always offering a solution immediately can be a real turn-off for the child. There are times in life when each of us merely wants to feel that someone is on our side. Watch the reaction of your kids carefully, and you will learn to gauge when and when not to offer solutions or empathy.

To use empathy effectively, mean what you say. Use a soft, comforting voice, and watch the child's reaction. Offer to help, if necessary, and follow up. If you know a child was feeling depressed, check later to see if he or she is doing better. Remember how you felt in similar situations, what you did to escape those emotional ruts, and how other people helped you (or the ways you wanted someone to help).

Empathy can show young people how much you genuinely care. It is an essential factor in building relationships.

Praise

> *Nothing improves a person's hearing*
> *more than praise.*

More people need to realize the power of praise. Praise is nourishment. It helps children grow emotionally just as food helps them grow physically.

Part of the problem is that we have been programmed to recognize mistakes and weaknesses, not good deeds and strengths. For example, in the business world there is something called the "3:11" rule. Simply stated, it means that if you go to a restaurant and have a good meal, you're likely to tell three people about it. If you have a bad meal, you're likely to tell 11. In other words, our society tends to focus on the negative.

Now is the time to "upgrade" the way we treat other people, to start noticing and praising the positive. Using praise is especially important when you are working with kids. Learning how to praise effectively works wonders.

Let's look at some guidelines for making praise work:

- Praise the behavior in a way that the child understands. Avoid using general phrases that leave your praise open to interpretation. Give young people enough information for them to fully understand how or why they should continue their good behavior. It's best to specifically describe the behavior you want to see again. Say things such as, "You did a great job finishing your homework on time," or "Thanks for saying 'Hi' to me when you walked in the classroom. You used a pleasant voice." In this way, children will know what behaviors you approve of and want to see again.

- Be specific at first, and gradually move to general praise as your youth internalize positive behaviors. When a child demonstrates a behavior or skill frequently, too much specific praise can be nonreinforcing or irritating, and can even appear to be condescending. Sometimes, a simple statement like "Good job," is enough to make the youth feel valued for their special qualities. Kids progress at different rates, and your praise should be adjusted according to their age and ability to understand. Also, you can show appreciation by pointing out a child's overall qualities – "You really stick with a task until it's done"; "You're very patient and understanding when someone asks a lot of questions about something you already understand"; or "You're a sensitive person." Respect the uniqueness of your kids and recognize what makes each of them feel worthwhile and accepted.

• Be brief. Too much praise sounds phony. Simply state the behavior in age-appropriate, specific, and understandable words: "Good job of putting the cleaning supplies away. Everything is where it's supposed to be," or "Your essay was very descriptive, and you used great examples."

• Be enthusiastic! Praise must have some emotion behind it. You should feel good that your youth has met your expectations. Show it!

• Give praise immediately. If you see a positive behavior, don't wait to praise it. Delayed praise loses its zing. Just think what could happen if you told a loved one that he or she "looked good yesterday." The reaction might be, "What! I don't look good today?"

- Smile. Acceptance of a behavior comes through loud and clear when praise is accompanied by a smiling face.

- Give praise at an appropriate time and in ways the kids like. We just said to give praise immediately, but there may be situations when it's better to wait. For example, some kids don't like to be praised in front of others; it embarrasses them. Some kids like a "thumbs up" or a simple head nod showing approval better than words. Some kids like loud, boisterous, cheerleading-like praise. Others like a softer, more sensitive style. Find out what works for each youth in order to make the praise meaningful.

- Use appropriate body language. Look at the child, and stand or sit on the same level as the child. Don't hover over young people; they'll feel intimidated or controlled even if what you have to say is good. A pat on the back, a wink, a "high-five" – each can be very encouraging and signal a job well done.

- Don't compare kids or bring up past inappropriate behaviors. Do say, "That was a super catch you made." Don't say, "You're the best player on the team." Do say, "What a great job you did cleaning your room." Don't say, "Your room looks good. Why can't you do that all the time? Ivanna does."

- Kids shouldn't feel that they have to be the "best" at something in order to be accepted. Instead, they should be encouraged to make the most of their talents without becoming obsessed with the need to be "Number One." While healthy competition allows children to strive to improve their talents, overcompetitiveness creates ill feelings between kids. And for some, it sets an unachievable standard. Comparing kids is a sure-fire way to cause jealousy or resentment. Often, you can praise the effort as well as the accomplishment because not all children will excel at a task.

- Be sincere. Kids can spot phoniness immediately. Don't give praise if you don't mean it.

Listening

Hearing is an ability; listening is an art.

The skill of listening cannot be overemphasized. Much of our communication with other people is accomplished without saying a word. Listening demonstrates caring, interest, and warmth.

Children need to have someone listen to what they have to say. Many kids have not yet learned how to express themselves. At times, they feel one way but their words say something else. By listening carefully, you can pick up on cues that indicate what is troubling a young person. Sometimes, you may have to restate or rephrase what the youth said. You can ask questions that may help a young person find a solution to a problem. You can label feelings and emotions and explain how they affect behavior. Sometimes kids say "off-the-wall" things just to get our attention or indicate that something is bothering them. A simple "Would you like to talk about it?" can open the doors to a meaningful interaction. A great deal of teaching can be done if you are attentive and really listen.

Here are some important elements of good listening:

- Make sure your voice tone matches the message you are trying to give. This means being aware of how loud or soft and how slow or fast your conversation is. Often, young people will remember the way you said something longer and better than the actual words you said. For example, speaking softly and slowly may help soothe an angry child. An enthusiastic voice may encourage a child to "keep up the good work" or try harder. A sarcastic voice shows that you aren't sincere, regardless of what you say. Therefore, make sure your voice sends the right message.

- Physical touch is a powerful communicator. It shows warmth and acceptance. A pat on the back or an arm around the shoulder can comfort a sad or lonely child. Shaking hands or "giving five" can show your approval and satisfaction.

    Of course, touch can be misused and misunderstood. Touch should never be threatening, intimidating, or sexual in nature. It is crucial that you give kids their "personal space" because it shows your respect for their right to privacy.

- Looking at the child is very important. If you never look up from your book or papers, a young person will think you don't care. You also will miss an opportunity to watch the child's facial expressions – keys that help you determine what the child is feeling.

As a form of nonverbal expression, "the eyes have it."

• Be understanding. Kids live in their "kid world," just as we live in our "adult world." Those worlds don't always exist in perfect harmony. Often, when kids attempt to explain a dilemma in their lives, adults say things like, "That's not a problem. Wait until you're older; you'll know what real problems are." That's the same as saying, "Go away, kid. You're bothering me."

   Try to see things from the child's perspective. If a young person feels like sharing something with you, listen attentively. In fact, you should feel good that he or she trusted you enough to ask for your help. All ages and developmental stages bring new problems into a young person's life. Be understanding and listen carefully. What may seem like a minor problem to you, could be monumental to a child.

• Use facial expressions and body language that show you are interested. Smile, nod your head, and keep your arms and hands relaxed. Face the child, and stand or sit close by while still giving him or her some personal space. Your facial expressions and body posture indicate your willingness to listen.

Of all the things you wear, your expression is the most important.

Thoughtfulness

It is one of the most beautiful compensations of this life that no man can sincerely help another without helping himself.

Don't you like it when someone unexpectedly does something nice for you? It's a boost to your day, isn't it? One of the biggest factors in developing relationships is thoughtfulness – doing or saying nice things for someone else. It takes very little time or effort, but it is so powerful.

Little acts of kindness mean a great deal. A note or card, a phone call, a compliment, a smile or word of sympathy, remembering a birthday or special occasion – all bring a smile to another person's face. Kids need to know how much you care, and these small acts of kindness help make you a welcome and necessary part of their lives. Your kindness also shows kids the importance of helping others. That is a very valuable lesson, indeed.

Give and Take

Healthy relationships are not one-sided. By using the qualities discussed earlier, you are giving your kids a good example to follow. But when you are just beginning to develop a relationship with younger kids, you will need to take the initiative. In fact, sometimes it may seem as though you're doing all of the giving. That's to be expected. However, as the bonds between you and your kids grow, the kids will learn to reciprocate your warmth and concern. You may, in fact, be one of the few people from whom they gain strength and acceptance.

Relationships thrive when there is equal give and take. However, you are well aware that there are many young people who think only of themselves. There could be many reasons for that but one obvious culprit is the kind of messages that tell them that they can buy an "identity" in the local shopping mall. Buy the image and you'll be cool; without it, you're nothing. So, time and again, kids have it pounded in their brains: Look out only for yourself and grab all you can. Unfortunately, that message is light years away from the real meaning of a good life.

We too often love things and use people when we should be using things and loving people.

Kids need to learn how fulfilling it is to help others, that it is one of the greatest joys in life. In other words, they need to learn how to move from being self-centered to other-centered and that they should treat others as they want to be treated. The Golden Rule must be lived, not just learned. Only then will kids begin to understand what happiness and a good life are all about.

There are many ways to get this point across. Read stories that illustrate compassion and helpfulness. Arrange activities that involve teamwork and cooperation. Talk about current events where people helped those who are less fortunate or lent a helping hand in time of sorrow or disaster.

Kids have to learn to give; that means giving of their time, their compassion, and themselves. Encourage them to volunteer to help at a youth or homeless shelter, work at an event like the Special Olympics, or visit a nursing home. Point out situations where they could do something nice for a classmate or friend, help a neighbor, or listen and understand when someone is depressed. These are the things that show kids that we all should be united in a relationship of caring, sharing, and helping. Those are gifts that you can give your kids that will last a lifetime.

Real happiness is more of a habit than a goal,
more of an attitude than an attainment.

The Importance of Building Strong Relationships

Without a relationship built on respect and trust, caregivers have to rely on authority and control. This creates an environment that is ripe for conflicts between you and your kids. Conversely, healthy relationships give a sense of family and community. It is possible to treat each young person as an individual while providing reasonable guidelines and expectations for everyone. Participating together in activities and discussion, sharing ideas, writing personal perspectives, and trading opinions can be valuable tools that build a warm and nurturing environment. When kids feel a sense of belonging and teamwork, there also will be less disruption and resistance. This allows you to concentrate on teaching and reinforcing the skills they need to learn.

Relationships are not visible or concrete, so they're sometimes hard to analyze. Developing a relationship is like building a house – you need a firm foundation, a good set of tools, and a dedicated routine. But it's also different. Each day you can see the progress on a house; it's much more difficult to see progress in a relationship. A house will be completed one day, just the way it was drawn up in the blueprints. In contrast, relationships are dynamic; they are going somewhere and changing all the time. They can get richer, grow old, end completely, begin anew, get better or get bitter – all depending on what we do to make them change. And what you see is not always what you get. There are no "relationship guarantees" that ensure customer satisfaction.

When most people think of good relationships, they think of happy times when everyone is getting along well. Or they remember the sad times when someone comforted them or helped them cope. The idea of good relationships can elicit many different emotions and perceptions. Therefore, as someone charged with the responsibility of helping young people, you must be able to deal with these moments along the way. If you form strong relationships with your kids, you also are much more likely to be able to defuse a potential powder keg of harmful emotions during angry times. When you learn to replace harmful behaviors that adults sometimes engage in – yelling, punishing, cajoling, or threatening – with helpful self-control techniques, it does wonders for calming an upset child. And it actually strengthens the relationship instead of tearing it down, as an angry response might do.

The relationship qualities that we have discussed here really work. Caregivers at Boys Town have learned this firsthand through their experiences with kids who were once angry, sullen, lazy, or withdrawn, and who now use prosocial skills to turn their lives around. These young people were able to accomplish this feat because the teachers, counselors, and other adults who were responsible for them learned how to promote positive relationship qualities in a natural way. It wasn't easy for some of these adults. We all know that it's hard to "teach an old dog new tricks." That certainly was true for some of the adults we worked with. But they found that they had to change their old behaviors and attitudes before they could change the behaviors and attitudes of the kids in their care. By consistently being aware of opportunities where they could teach and use positive relationship qualities, they found out how effective they could be in changing kids' behaviors. That's not the only good news. These qualities don't work just with young people; they work with everyone. People can learn to behave in ways that make them enjoyable to be around.

How do you know if you are establishing a positive, healthy relationship with a young person? Not all of the signals are direct and obvious; sometimes you will have to read the subtle cues your kids give you through their behavior. These could be physical actions like looking at you, looking down or away, or rolling their eyes. Other behaviors include facial expressions, voice tone, inflection, and body language. Also, after you have taught and modeled certain behaviors, look to see if the child is using what you are teaching about relationships. If the child is copying the qualities you are displaying, it means that he or she is internalizing those behaviors. If you aren't seeing the desired behaviors, determine what you could do differently, and adjust your behavior and teaching accordingly. However, you must be patient; changes will not occur overnight. It takes time and a consistent effort on your part. But these relationship qualities really work if you give them a chance.

Summary

Caregivers touch the minds and hearts of the young people in their care and are a source of enormous influence. The motivation and inspiration given to youth by a competent and compassionate teacher is a special gift.

Positive relationships take many forms. A true, meaningful relationship cannot exist without warmth and a genuine sense of caring by the people involved. This type of relationship is not always easy to create and develop, especially for people who lack some of the skills and qualities we have discussed. But for everyone who works with or cares for kids – parents, teachers, counselors, youth -care professionals, and others – these skills and qualities must either be part or become part of their personalities. Adults cannot make a lasting difference in a child's life if there is no personal connection. And this connection must be nurtured if it is to grow into a rich, rewarding relationship for the child and the adult.

Teaching skills and building relationships are the two primary ingredients to having happy and successful children, children who will grow up with positive feelings about themselves and their role in the world. Teaching is what helps kids learn new ways of thinking, new ways of feeling, and new ways of behaving. Teaching gives kids the skills they need to become responsible and independent people.

Strong relationships create a bond of trust between you and your kids. It makes them feel connected and worthwhile. Kids are more likely to learn from and try to imitate a person who is warm, fun to be with, and reliable. Developing healthy emotional bonds with the kids in your care is crucial to their eventual success in school, at home, and in society as a whole. Through your care and compassion, they will learn what makes healthy relationships and carry those skills into adulthood.

Quality Teaching

When Jennifer was 10, her dad started having long talks with her about being able to think for herself. He would tell her how important it was to assess a situation, consider the facts, and make a decision. Dad reasoned that by teaching Jennifer to rely on her thinking skills, she would always make the right choices as she grew up. These discussions continued through grade school, junior high, and high school. By the time Jennifer was in her teens, she had learned to look at situations from many different angles and come up with options for how to respond or behave. The problem was that Jennifer's dad didn't teach her much about appropriate feelings and behaviors; he just figured she'd learn from her mistakes. When Jennifer sometimes made the wrong choices, the results were disastrous.

✳   ✳   ✳

The Smiths always tried to make sure their son, Toby, felt good about himself. Whenever Toby made a mistake, one of them was right there to tell the boy that it wasn't his fault or that Dad or Mom would make it better. Toby grew up thinking he was someone special because his parents never raised their voices or took things away from him when he misbehaved. He quickly learned that he could do pretty much whatever he wanted because his parents would bend over backwards to make sure he never felt bad or unhappy. The Smiths even went so far as to argue with teachers and the principal at Toby's school when he got bad grades or broke the rules; they said punishing Toby would damage his self-esteem. Toby enjoyed all the attention, but he never really learned much about thinking for himself or taking responsibility for his behaviors.

✳   ✳   ✳

A typical day at the Jones house started with a whistle blast and a mad dash by four kids to make their beds, get dressed, and rush to the breakfast table by 6:30 a.m. Dad Jones believed in obedience, respect, and efficiency, and when he blew that whistle every morning, it was time for the kids to snap to and hit the floor running. Following the family's strict rules was mandatory for the Jones kids. The consequences were simple: Do what you're supposed to do and you stay out of trouble; mess up and you clean the driveway with a toothbrush. There was no time for hugging or other mushy displays of affection, and Dad always made it clear that he would do the thinking for the family. As the years went by, he always took pride in the fact that his kids were the best-behaved students in school and that they could be counted on to do what they were told without back talk or questions. It didn't matter much to him that the kids didn't have many friends or that they rarely told him that they loved him. Discipline was the key to success, and his kids were going to be successful. He was never was able to see that his children had become robots who were " programmed" to obey.

✳ ✳ ✳

Thoughts. Feelings. Behaviors. When you get down to the basics of teaching children, these are the three elements that command center stage. Ideally, there is a positive, consistent connection among these elements when a child must decide how to behave; the child has positive thoughts and feelings about a situation, and subsequently engages in a positive behavior. Sometimes, however, kids engage in a positive behavior regardless of what they are thinking or feeling. While there is an inconsistency here, children who can do this have

55

learned an important value – that they should behave appropriately because it's the right thing to do.

The examples you have just read may seem extreme in their depiction of what happens when parents decide to confine their teaching to just one of these elements. The purpose here is not to criticize these approaches, but rather, to show how teaching in only one area can undermine the efforts of even the most loving and caring parent or caregiver.

The goal of teaching children is to help them change themselves for the better. This teaching takes place at home, in school, and, for troubled or at-risk children, in treatment or youth-care settings. Adults have a responsibility to find the best ways to equip children with the skills and knowledge they need in order to succeed in society. This is true whether you are a parent, a schoolteacher, or a child-care professional. At Boys Town, we have focused our efforts on helping youth learn behaviors that can help them be successful. At the same time, however, we empower youth to make the connection between their thoughts and feelings and the way they behave. The thoughts and feelings a youth might have do not always lead to the appropriate or desired behavior, and a positive behavior does not always reflect positive thoughts or feelings. However, as you will see, consistency in the way teaching and learning occurs is the measure of true success when helping children to better themselves. This success is evident when children can consistently use socially acceptable behaviors as they assume control of their own lives.

It is important to remember that learning does not occur in a vacuum. Every situation a youth faces is different, and every event in his or her environment affects how the youth thinks, feels, and acts. This includes the relationships a youth has with adults, the youth's age and developmental level, the youth's life experiences, and other factors that make the youth who he or she is. That is why the most effective teaching comes from both the head and the heart. An adult must have a plan that gives his or her teaching structure and substance. This is the competence, the "head." There also must be a warmth and sincerity that enables an adult to build a relationship with a youth. This is the "heart," the compassion that creates a natural and caring connection between the teacher and the youth. Teaching without compassion is pure manipulation; teaching without competence is pure sentimentality. Kids are human beings, and the adults who teach them must bring a humanity to that task.

The purpose of this article is to help you become better at teaching children by using the best qualities of different teaching approaches. We'll discuss how people teach and what is important in helping kids learn new skills and behaviors. We'll also outline a proven teaching method that enables adults to incorporate warmth, flexibility, and a naturalness of manner that children enjoy and respond to, and empowers youth to change for the better.

You may have considerable experience working with kids, or you may be just getting started. Whatever your situation, it is your responsibility to teach kids how to replace negative behaviors with positive behaviors that will help them meet their needs. This is valuable information that can make your work more satisfying.

What Kind of Teacher Are You?

It could be argued that there are as many teaching styles as there are adult caregivers. But while it's true that anyone who cares for or works with children has an individual teaching style, most adults tend to fall in one of two camps regarding discipline and relationship-building.

Some say that it is important for adults to have strong relationships with kids. They feel that providing firm discipline detracts from relation-ships and that if you just "love" kids enough, you can overcome their problems.

Others take an opposite stance. They say that kids today need firm discipline. They feel that having a relationship with kids that is too strong, warm, and caring can create a harmful situation. They reason that when this happens, the child never learns how to respond to authority or social situations.

At Boys Town, we have found that both relationship-building and teaching are fundamental components of helping children. In fact, they are the highlights of our Model of care.

Using these two qualities as criteria, the diagram on page 61 shows how most people fall into one of four teaching categories. In the first category, people who have low teaching skills and low relationship-building skills are going to be poor teachers. They spend little time or energy on teaching kids skills, and it would be very difficult for them to reach kids in a meaningful way.

The next category includes those who have low relationship-building skills but high teaching skills. These people often appear uncaring, cold, and punitive toward children. They seldom give praise and constantly find fault. Kids see little benefit in "becoming like them," and are not able to learn and maintain life skills these people might try to teach.

While kids initially may be more comfortable with adults in the next category – high relationship-building skills and low teaching skills – they often have a difficult time respecting them. These adults can develop warm, caring relationships with children, but they aren't able to teach concepts or values such as self-discipline and responsibility. The kids might have fun being around them, but when the kids mess up because they lack skills, these adults respond with disappointment and an attitude of "I loved you and trusted you, and look what you did." This doesn't help the kids, and some may not feel "safe," because these adults have a hard time setting clear tolerances and expectations for the child.

In our experience, men and women who are most successful in helping children are those who fall into the fourth category – high relationship-building skills and high teaching skills. They enjoy children, and kids feel good being around them. They take an interest in a child and become strong role models. They can remain calm and deal with negative or unpleasant situations without getting angry or upset. They also set clear expectations and consistently follow through with consequences for positive and negative behaviors. It is easier for a child to be successful if he or she is taught skills consistently in an atmosphere of warmth, caring, and acceptance. Children also find it easier to feel safe because they know they are with people who will protect them. It is easier for them to maintain the behaviors they learn because they have good role models whom they want to please and emulate.

Teaching Skills

	High	*Low*
Building Relationships *High*	Warm, caring, enjoys being around kids, sincere interest in children, strong role model, sets clear expectations, protective	Warm, caring, kids enjoy being around, disappointed in kids when they mess up, doesn't set clear expectations and boundaries, kids might not feel safe
Low	Uncaring, cold, punitive toward kids, gives praise infrequently, constantly finds fault with kids, poor role model	Spends little time teaching kids, no warmth or caring skills, little or no positive influence on children, insincere, cold

61

It's easy to see why the most effective teaching – the teaching that really reaches kids and stays with them as they grow and face new situations – is both caring and grounded in proven methods. Some people are born with the ability to develop healthy, helpful relationships with children, while others must work hard on developing their interpersonal skills. Some people can easily learn teaching methods and techniques that work, while others might struggle to learn how to apply such methods in their work with children. Whatever the case, adults who take on the responsibility of helping children have a duty to make themselves better teachers. Otherwise, they are cheating the kids who turn to them for a better life.

Thoughts, Feelings, Actions

At the beginning of this article, we presented scenarios in which parents focused their teaching and child-rearing skills on only one area of development – thinking, feeling, or behaving. In each of those examples, the parents failed to teach the children that a person's thoughts, feelings, and behaviors are connected and dependent on each other. For example, a person who wakes up to the ring of the alarm clock at 6 a.m. may think it's too early to get up for work. He may even think the boss won't miss him if he skips a day. Then the person may lie in bed for a few minutes, telling himself that he doesn't feel like working. But knowing that he has to go to work, the person gets up and starts getting ready. After a shower and breakfast, the person may start to feel better about the day ahead; his thinking and attitude change, resulting in the behavior of being to work on time. A number of factors came into play – the possibility of a negative consequence (getting fired) for not going to work, the person's sense of responsibility and loyalty to his employer, the positive consequence of earning money, the fact that the person enjoys being with his co-workers. This person was able to assess all these factors, determine how they made him feel, and then behave in a responsible manner. It doesn't matter that the entire sequence began with a negative thought and a negative feeling; the changes in thoughts and attitudes that occurred eventually led to a positive behavior.

This is what children need to learn from adults, whether the adults are parents, teachers, or child-care professionals. At Boys Town, we've found that it is most effective to start this process by teaching new, appropriate behaviors. Behaviors are what people are judged by; one can't always know what a person is thinking or feeling. Along those same lines, behaviors are visible indicators that a child either doesn't know what to do or has learned a "wrong" behavior. They "tell" a caregiver when teaching is necessary, something a child's thoughts and feelings can't do. Because behaviors occur all the time, a caregiver has many opportunities to teach and reinforce what a child has learned. Behaviors also determine more than anything how we get along with others. Children must learn that their behavior affects others and that they can improve their chances for success by using behaviors that are pleasant and socially acceptable.

As part of this process, adults also must teach children how to internalize and generalize the skills they learn. Internalizing means that children make new skills and behaviors a permanent part of their lives in order to be able to use them in the future. This usually has been accomplished when a child's thoughts and feelings reflect the teaching that has occurred. Generalizing means that a child is able to use a skill or behavior in a variety of situations. This is where the "thinking" part of our three-pronged teaching approach comes into play. Kids who simply react to a situation, usually with inappropriate behavior, must learn how to sort through a situation and decide which skill or behavior will work best. This is a difficult step for kids whose needs have been ignored. But once a child makes headway in this area, he or she has taken a big step toward taking responsibility for and control of his or her life.

It is unreasonable to think that children, or adults for that matter, are going to have positive thoughts, feelings, and behaviors in every situation. It is possible for a person to behave appropriately and still have negative thoughts and negative feelings about a situation. A person also could have positive thoughts and feelings, and still fail to use the right or socially acceptable behavior. In fact, many combinations of negative or positive thoughts, feelings, and behaviors are possible. The point here is that you should not expect perfection from children in the way they think, feel, or act. Rather, the goal should be to teach them how and why negative behaviors can harm them or cause them trouble, and how using positive behaviors can benefit them or others. This teaching approach makes children active participants in the learning process and prompts them to think and express their emotions. Progress is measured by behavioral changes, but the child also is challenged to change on an intellectual and emotional level.

Here are two examples that illustrate the connection between thoughts, feelings, and behaviors. The first example is positive; the second is negative.

A child who knows his mother's birthday is coming up thinks it would be nice to do something to make her day special. Acting on his feelings of love for his mom, the boy sits down and makes her a card that reads, "Happy Birthday to the Best Mom in the World." In this situation, the child reacted to his mother's birthday with positive thinking, feelings, and behavior.

A girl is walking down the hallway at school. As she passes two other girls, she sees one whisper something to the other. Thinking that the two are talking about her, the girl starts feeling angry. She stops, walks back to the pair, and slugs the girl who was whispering. Having acted against her "antagonist," she continues down the hall. In this case, the girl reacted with negative thoughts to seeing two girls talking, which led to negative feelings and negative behavior.

At this point, you may be asking some questions: How does one go about teaching so that all these areas are covered? What do I do to reach the children I want to help? How do I improve my relationship-building skills and teaching skills to be the most effective teacher I can be? In the next section we will try to answer these questions.

Corrective Teaching

Teaching can occur anytime. Children are constantly asking questions or are in need of instructions for how to do something. Adults respond to these opportunities by sharing their experience, knowledge, and abilities. That's how children learn and grow socially and emotionally. However, much of the teaching adults do is in response to a child's failure to do what he or she should do or to a child's misbehavior. This type of teaching requires a process that provides both structure and flexibility. Structure helps make the teaching consistent and effective and ensures that critical components are presented. Flexibility allows the person who is doing the teaching to modify the process to fit the child's needs and the circumstances of the situation. This means that simple skills and complex skills can be taught using the same basic method.

At Boys Town, this process is called Corrective Teaching®. This proven teaching method is comprised of three central concepts: Description, Relationship, and Consequence. The Description concept includes describing a behavior in words or actions, role-playing, and practice. The Relationship concept involves using friendliness, warmth, and pleasantness, and showing genuine concern for the youth. It also involves helping the child to feel good about himself or herself. The Consequence concept includes praise, feedback, and, obviously, a consequence for the inappropriate behavior. Effective teaching requires a balance among these three concepts.

As we discussed earlier, adults who are the best teachers of children have high teaching skills and high relationship-building skills. In Corrective Teaching, the Consequence and Description concepts encompass the elements of effective teaching skills. The Relationship concept contains the elements for high relationship-building skills.

Within each of these concepts are components that give structure to the teaching process. Here are those components and their definitions:

Description (words and deeds)

- **Description of inappropriate behavior** – Telling the child what he or she did wrong or failed to do. It should be simple and brief, so that the child can understand it, and it can be presented in words or actions (a demonstration).

- **Description of appropriate behavior** – A simple and brief explanation of a behavior the child should use in place of the inappropriate behavior. Again, it is important to make sure your words or actions fit the child's age or developmental level.

- **Rationale** – Why the child should change his or her behavior. For younger children, this reason should tell them how they will personally benefit from using a new behavior. Older children can be told how using a new behavior will be good for them and/or others.

- **Practice** – An opportunity for the child to use a new behavior or skill in a made-up situation before he or she has to use it in real life. This gives the child a chance to be successful and gain confidence.

Relationship

- **Initial praise/empathy** – Beginning the teaching in a positive way. It lets the child know that someone cares enough to help, and recognizes the child for some positive behavior he or she is using.

- **Rationale** – Explaining the good that will come out of using a new behavior. This helps improve relationships because the child can see that the adult wants the child to receive some kind of benefit.

- **Acknowledgment** – Asking the child if he or she understands what is being taught. This should be used throughout the teaching.

- **Praise** – Recognizing the child for doing something right. This shows the youth that the adult isn't focusing only on the negative, and that the adult has confidence that the youth can be successful.

- **Warmth** (quality components) – Showing the youth throughout the teaching that he or she is important, loved, and wanted. Smiles, pats on the back, laughter, and a friendly facial expression are just a few of these components. It's also necessary to stay calm; this allows the adult to focus on the issue and helps the child to stay calm. (See the article, "The Vital Signs of Relationships for Caregivers.")

Consequence

- **Initial praise/empathy** – Usually the adult's first statement when he or she sees that teaching is needed. The adult's attention and the time a youth must spend during the teaching can be considered a consequence to the behavior.

- **Consequence** – Taking away something the child likes or giving the child something he or she doesn't like. For example, a parent might tell a child that he can't go to a friend's house because the child didn't clean his room. A youth-care worker might have a child do an extra chore for not following an instruction. (Boys Town uses Motivation Systems in which youth earn negative points for inappropriate behavior and positive points for appropriate behavior. Positive points can be exchanged for privileges.) It is important when giving consequences that the child understands that it was his or her behavior that earned the consequence and that he or she is responsible for that behavior.

- **Feedback** – Telling the child how he or she is doing as the teaching takes place. This is especially useful when the child practices a new skill or behavior.

- **Praise** – Recognizing the child's efforts to learn and practice a new behavior. This can be used anytime a youth responds to teaching in a positive way.

To better understand Corrective Teaching and its components, let's look at its use in terms of how a carpenter builds a house. When construction begins, it is important that the house has a strong foundation. The carpenter will work carefully, making measurements and deciding which tools or combination of tools will work best. Initially, the carpenter may use all of his tools as he puts in the floor and frames the walls. Once the foundation and framework are in place, he will start building onto it, perhaps using fewer tools to put up walls and braces that hold joints together. At a certain point, the work becomes more routine, and the carpenter knows exactly what tools to use and when to use them to keep the construction going. During the entire project, the carpenter is checking and fine-tuning his work.

In teaching, the teacher is like the carpenter, and the Corrective Teaching components are like his tools. An adult caregiver must first lay a foundation of trust and respect in order to establish a strong relationship. This is accomplished through meeting the emotional needs of a child and creating an environment where the child knows he or she will be cared for, protected, and loved. Obviously, this relationship should be established quickly and naturally between parents and their children. But in education or treatment settings, adults often will be meeting for the first time the youth in their care. These situations will require an assessment of such things as the child's age and developmental level, which skills are absent, and past responses to consequences and confrontation.

As work continues on the foundation, the caregiver also must start teaching to problem behaviors using the tools he or she brings to the job. At first, the caregiver will use them all. This will establish a consistent framework for teaching that will help the youth understand the caregiver's expectations. Then, as the youth becomes familiar and more comfortable with the teaching process and shows progress, the caregiver can begin to teach using fewer tools. This is especially true for behaviors that have required numerous Teaching Interactions®. After a while, youth know what they've done and what they should have done, and caregivers can modify their teaching to reflect this progress. That means using fewer components or using them in different combinations.

Over time, a skillful caregiver will be able to determine exactly how to approach each teaching opportunity and which components are necessary. Ideally, the youth will begin to make the new learned behaviors part of his or her daily life and will know how to apply new skills to a variety of situations. The youth also is learning a different way of thinking and feeling because of the relationship-building and teaching that has occurred. The caregiver becomes more natural in his or her teaching, and can now teach in a less-structured manner while still achieving the same positive results. And, most importantly, the youth and the caregiver have benefited from their experience together.

The longer a caregiver works with a youth, the more natural teaching should become. By selectively using the components of Corrective Teaching, a caregiver continues to provide structure while capitalizing on his or her personal qualities to strengthen the relationship. The result is a positive change in the child's thoughts, feelings, and behaviors, and an overall change for the better.

With these concept areas as guideposts, and the components serving as the "path" teaching should follow, let's look at examples of how an adult would teach a child the skill of making an apology. In the first example, a mother has just started using Corrective Teaching with her child.

Example 1 – Ten-year-old Tim is playing with his eight-year-old cousin, Tina, in the back yard. They get into an argument over whose turn it is to use the tire swing. Tim pushes Tina down and jumps in the swing. Tina goes inside crying, and tells Tim's Mom what happened. Mom calls Tim in, and they sit down on the living room couch.

Mom: *"Tim, thanks for coming in right away and sitting down on the couch.* (Praise) *We need to talk about what happened in the yard just now. It was wrong for you to push Tina down so you could have the swing. You're a lot bigger than she is, and you could have hurt her.* (Description of the Inappropriate Behavior) *Do you understand?"* (Request for Acknowledgment)

Tim: *"Yeah, I understand. But it was my turn to swing."*

Mom: *"Even if it was your turn, pushing her down was no way to settle the argument. You should have tried to work things out so that you both got a turn, or come in and asked me for help.* (Description of Appropriate Behavior)

That way, you wouldn't end up doing something that could hurt the other person and get you in trouble. (Rationale) *Okay?"*

Tim: *"Okay."*

Mom: *"Now, for pushing Tina, you've earned an hour in your room.* (Consequence) *Before you go there, you have to apologize to her."*

Tim: *"Do I have to?"*

Mom: *"Tim, that's the right thing to do when you push or hit someone. Do you know how to make an apology?"*

Tim: *"I don't know. I just say 'I'm sorry.'"*

Mom: *"That's important. But there's a little more to it than that. When you make an apology, you should look at the other person, say you're sorry, and tell the person what you're sorry for. You should be serious and sincere. Do you know what sincere means?"*

Tim: *"It means I should say it like I really mean it."*

Mom: *"Very good. That's exactly what it means. And you shouldn't make excuses. That shows that you take responsibility for what you did. Understand?"*

Tim: *"Yes."*

Mom: *"Okay, let's practice what you're going to do and say. Pretend that I'm Tina and that you're apologizing for pushing me down."*

Tim: (looking at Mom) *"Tina, I'm sorry I pushed you down when we were arguing about the swing. I won't do it again."* (Practice)

Mom: *"That was great! You looked at me and used a sincere voice. And you told me exactly what you were apologizing for.* (Praise and Feedback) *Now let's go find Tina so you can talk to her. Then you can go to your room."*

Now let's look at a similar scenario in a family where the parents have been using Corrective Teaching for several months.

Example 2 – Dad is asking his 13-year-old daughter Jenny to apologize for taking a CD from her sister's room without permission.

Dad: *"Jenny, I need to talk to you for a minute. Carrie just told me that you took a CD from her bedroom without asking if you could take it."* (Description of Inappropriate Behavior)

Jenny: *"But Dad, Allison was here, and I wanted her to hear this good song."*

Dad: *"I realize you wanted to listen to the CD and that it was right there in Carrie's room* (Empathy), *but you still need to ask for permission when you want to borrow something that doesn't belong to you.* (Description of Appropriate Behavior) *When you ask, the person is more likely to give you what you want* (Rationale). *We've been over this before so you know that. For taking the CD without permission, you've earned two extra chores this week – doing the laundry and dusting.* (Consequence) *Now I'd like you to go apologize to Carrie. Remember what to do?"*

Jenny: *"Yes. I'll look at her, use a sincere voice, and tell her I'm sorry for taking the CD out of her room without asking. Okay?"*

Dad: *"All right. Thanks for going over the steps.* (Feedback) *I think Carrie's in the kitchen."*

78

In the first situation, the parent used every teaching component. This provided the structure that is necessary when teaching to a child who is just becoming familiar with a new way of learning how to correct inappropriate behaviors. In the second situation, in which the youth was familiar with her father's teaching, the father was able to get his point across in a brief conversation. In both cases, the parents dealt with the inappropriate behaviors with effective teaching, and taught a skill. This illustrates how flexible the Corrective Teaching method is, and how it can be modified as a child makes progress and becomes familiar with expected behaviors and skills.

Teaching to One Child

Every child is different. Each has his or her own strengths, weaknesses, and way of looking at the world. That's why the teaching you do – whether you are a parent, an educator, a child-care professional, or in some other position where you work with children – must be individualized to fit each child's needs.

Several factors come into play here. (See the charts on page 81.) Depending on your situation, some will have more relevance than others. For example, parents have a relationship with their

79

children that is different from a relationship between a child and a staff member in a youth shelter. Schoolteachers must use their teaching skills under a different set of rules than those that govern a group home for troubled children. This is not to say that the teaching approaches and methods we've discussed won't work; it means only that each caregiver must look at these factors and modify how he or she teaches to each child.

The first factor to consider is the age of the child. Younger children respond best to teaching that is brief and specific. In other words, you must teach using easy-to-understand language and examples that are part of the child's world. Younger children don't have a long attention span, so it's important to get right to the point. Also, the younger a child is, the fewer times you will teach so that the child is not overwhelmed. As a child matures and is better able to understand and handle more complex skills, teaching can be done more frequently. The same generally holds true for children who have learning disabilities or mental or physical health problems.

This pattern usually changes as children get older and make progress in acquiring skills. Then, the number of Teaching Interactions can decrease and interactions can be shorter. When teaching is

Age of Child

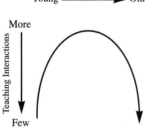

Skill Deficits

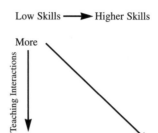

Developmental Stages

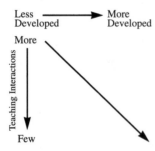

Length of Time in Program

Ratio of Staff to Kids

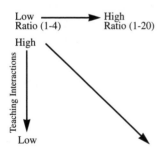

effective, children become more familiar with the behavior that is expected of them and begin to understand what happens when they don't meet expectations.

The number of skills a child has mastered also determines how and when teaching will occur. Caregivers will do more teaching with kids who have few skills; this is necessary in order to help them learn new skills as quickly as possible. On the other hand, children who have many skills and know how to use them require fewer Teaching Interactions. This also applies to the area of children's developmental stages. Children who are less mature may require more teaching; children who are more mature may require less teaching.

For youth-care programs, there are two main factors that determine the amount of teaching that occurs – the length of time a child has been in a program and the ratio of staff to children. The shorter the time a child has been in a program, the more teaching is necessary. This is because a child usually must learn a number of basic skills in order to function in the program and get the biggest benefit from it. A child who has been in a program for a while knows what behaviors are expected, and has been taught certain skills numerous times.

With staff ratios, staff will have more opportunities to teach when they are responsible for fewer children. A staff member who has four children in her care will have more time to teach than a staff member who is in charge of 15 children.

As we mentioned earlier, the relationship you have with a child will have the greatest impact on what direction your teaching takes. Teaching will be more structured and take more time at the beginning of a relationship with a child, but should become more natural and brief as the child learns new behaviors and skills.

In considering these factors, it is important to remember that these are general descriptions of how teaching occurs in different settings with different children. Caregivers must be flexible and able to recognize when their teaching should be modified.

Summary

In order for an adult to be an effective teacher, he or she must possess a number of positive qualities. Foremost among these qualities are teaching skills and relationship-building skills. A good teacher must be proficient in both areas – the ability to teach is not enough if a caregiver cannot estab-

lish a warm, caring relationship with a child; like-
wise, even the strongest relationship between a
caregiver and a child would be useless if the caregiver can not help the child learn new behaviors
that will bring about a positive change.

Another quality that is essential to teaching
is the ability to address children's needs in three
developmental areas – thinking, feeling, and behaving. There are many theories concerning how to
bring about meaningful, long-lasting changes in a
youth's behavior. Some concentrate only on changing the way a child thinks about his or her environment; others focus on making sure the child is emotionally healthy. Boys Town has found that changing behavior is the best starting place when working with young people. Behaviors are the visible
measure of a child's progress, and this area is the
easiest to focus on because behaviors indicate what
a child needs to learn. But we also believe that a
child's thoughts and feelings must be part of the
metamorphosis that a child undergoes as he or she
grows and learns. Our teaching methods are
designed to cover all three areas, so that children
derive the biggest benefit possible.

Corrective Teaching is a proven method for
helping youth replace inappropriate behaviors with
appropriate behaviors. Three concept areas –

Description, Relationship, and Consequence – comprise the Corrective Teaching Interaction. Within these areas are specific components that provide structure to the teaching process while developing and strengthening relationships. These components should be followed closely when a caregiver first starts working with a child. As teaching becomes more natural and the child becomes more responsive to the caregiver, the use of the components can be modified. The goal is threefold – to make teaching a natural, effective process; to empower the child to make new behaviors a permanent part of daily life (internalization); and to enable the child to use these behaviors and skills in many different situations (generalization).

Teaching children how to change for the better is an awesome responsibility. Every situation you face will pose a different, and often difficult, challenge. Having confidence in your abilities and tools, and constantly improving how you apply them in your work, will be the key to success for you and the children in your care.

Everyone who shoulders the responsibility of helping or caring for children has some ability to teach new skills and appropriate behaviors. Only when a person applies that ability in a compassionate and competent manner, with the best interests of the child at heart, can the desired results be achieved – a child who has learned not only how to behave differently but how to live differently.

Why Do Kids Misbehave?

To work effectively with youth in your care, it is important to understand why they sometimes explode in antagonistic, aggressive, and often violent ways toward themselves and others. Caregivers who are familiar with theories on aggression and anger are more likely to provide effective treatment that can help youth change these negative behaviors. Effective treatment also depends on understanding the origins of a youth's negative behavior and why and how it continues to be reinforced. When caregivers take the time to do their "homework" on these issues, they can more easily identify problems and possible solutions, which results in better care for the youth.

Learning as much as possible about negative youth behavior is especially important when teaching youth self-control strategies that can help them face stressful or adverse situations calmly and rationally. Before using Boys Town's method of Crisis Teaching (which will be discussed in the next article) to help youth change their behaviors for the better, it is essential to look at the theoretical foundation of its development.

The Boys Town Teaching Model and techniques for teaching self-control have been influenced by the research and theories of Gerald Patterson, and more recently, Nicholas Long. Through their research, Patterson and Long have developed theories that seek to explain how youth have learned to deal inappropriately with conflict, and how caregivers can effectively work with these youth.

The following material explains Patterson's "Coercion Process" and Long's "Conflict Cycle," two important elements in understanding why kids respond to some social situations with anger, aggression, and a loss of self-control. This information is presented as an introduction to the process of Crisis Teaching.

The Coercion Process –
Gerald Patterson

Coercion refers to the use of one or more aversive behaviors or acts by a youth in response to the behavior of another person who generally is an authority figure (e.g., mother, father, teacher, foster parent, or other caregiver). The authority figure then responds to the youth's inappropriate behavior in one of two ways, labeled by Patterson (1982) as "escape conditioning" or "negative synchronicity." The end result of both types of responses is the same: The youth's inappropriate behavior is reinforced. Over time, the youth is trained to use aversive behavior whenever he or she is confronted with conflict because this behavior inevitably gets the youth what he or she wants. This ugly cycle of reinforcing negative or aversive youth behavior through erroneous authority responses is called the "Coercion Process."

Socially skilled youth learn to use appropriate behaviors to resolve negative or unpleasant social situations. However, if children have not learned socially appropriate behaviors, they will develop coping mechanisms to overcome these deficiencies. Children who have not been taught appropriate social skills learn to use the response that works best for them in a given situation.

Children are extremely tuned in to their social environment and learn to match their behavior to inadequate parental discipline, lack of structure, and poor problem-solving abilities.

The following sections explain the concepts of escape conditioning and negative synchronicity, and present examples of each.

Escape Conditioning

In this scenario, the authority figure immediately gives in and submits to the youth's coercive attack or inappropriate behavior. Thus, the unpleasant interaction abruptly ends and the authority figure escapes any further offensive exchanges with the youth. Unfortunately, this only reinforces the youth's aversive behavior by teaching him or her that the authority figure will withdraw his or her aversive behaviors if the child's behavior escalates beyond "tolerable" limits.

Example – A father scolds his son for leaving his bike outside instead of putting it in the garage. The son responds by screaming at his father, "It's my bike. I can keep it where I want!" or "Get off my back. It's no problem!" Thus, the son screams excuses at his father (coercion) so that his father will stop scolding him. The father immediately ceases the scolding and walks away, escaping any further conflict with the son. The son does not have to put his bike away and has now learned that he can stop or avoid his father's scolding by screaming back at him.

Negative Synchronicity

In this situation, when a youth engages in an aversive or inappropriate behavior, the authority figure immediately responds with aversive behavior. The coercive youth, in turn, escalates the intensity of his or her negative behavior until he or she "out-punishes" the authority figure. Eventually, the youth's negative behavior intensifies to the point where the authority figure concedes and ends the interaction. Again, the authority figure's response reinforces the youth's negative behavior.

Patterson showed that members of clinic-referred families were entrenched in this type of behavior-reaction cycle, and were roughly twice as likely as members of "normal" families to respond in this combative interaction style.

Example – A mother comes home after a long day's work and begins scolding her daughter for her messy room. The daughter begins screaming excuses: "I already cleaned it yesterday!" or "It's my room. I can keep it the way I want it!" The mother angrily shouts back at the daughter, "I'm the boss in this house and you will do what I tell you! Get upstairs and clean that damn room!" The daughter increases the intensity of her aversive behavior by angrily shouting back at her mother, cursing, and roughly knocking some books off a table. In turn, the mother irately threatens to "ground" the daughter. Upping the ante, the daughter responds by aggressively walking toward her mother with clenched fists, angrily shouting, "I'll do what I want. If you don't like it, I'll kick your ass!" At this point, the mother backs away and leaves, ending the hostile exchange. The daughter has learned that by escalating the intensity of her negative behaviors, she can avoid cleaning her room and eventually stop her mother's own aversive behaviors.

Much of Patterson's research helps to explain many of the clinical problems, such as children's antisocial behavior, that caregivers see today in increasing numbers. Coercive children respond to authority figures by trying to "out-punish" them. In some families, these behaviors are reinforced so often that the coercive child actually runs the family and controls the social setting. If these youth do not receive consequences for their aversive behaviors, they continue to use them whenever they are confronted by someone. These behaviors eventually spill over into interactions with others – family members, teachers, and other kids – whom the coercive child tries to out-punish or out-intimidate.

The Conflict Cycle – Nicholas Long

Long believes that a crisis has its root cause in an unresolved incident. The incident arouses strong emotions in the youth and others who were involved, and even a minor incident can spiral into a major crisis.

According to Long, crisis is the product of a youth's stress that is kept alive by the actions and reactions of others. When a youth's feelings are aroused by stress, the youth learns to behave in ways that shield him or her from painful feelings. These behaviors are inappropriate, but they protect the youth from undesirable, distressing feelings. Others (parents, teachers, peers) perceive the youth's behavior as negative, and they respond in a negative fashion toward the youth. This negative response from others produces additional stress and the youth again reacts in an inappropriate manner to protect himself or herself from further hurtful feelings. If unbroken, this spiraling action-reaction cycle causes a minor incident to escalate into a crisis. This process is called the Conflict Cycle.

The Conflict Cycle follows this pattern: The first step is a stressful event (e.g., frustration, failure, rejection, and so on) that triggers a troubled youth's irrational or negative beliefs (e.g., "Nothing good ever happens to me!"; "Adults are out to get me!"). Negative thoughts determine and trigger negative feelings and anxieties, which drive the youth's inappropriate behavior. The inappropriate behaviors (e.g., yelling, screaming, threatening, sarcasm, refusing to speak, and so on) incite others, who not only pick up the youth's negative feelings but also frequently mirror the youth's negative behaviors. This adverse reaction by others increases the youth's stress, triggers more intense feelings, and drives more negative behavior. The youth's behavior leads to even more anger and frustration on the part of the people around him or her. This cycle continues until it escalates into a no-win power struggle. Long says: "Logic, caring, and compassion are lost, and the only goal is to win the power struggle."

In the end, the youth's irrational beliefs (e.g., "Nothing good ever happens to me!"; "Adults are out to get me!") that started the Conflict Cycle sequence are reinforced, and the youth has no reason to change or alter his or her irrational beliefs and inappropriate behaviors.

Here is an example of the Conflict Cycle. (The cycle is illustrated on the next page.)

Example – A youth is late for school and does not have a written excuse (EVENT creating STRESS – Cycle 1 Begins). School policy states that students must stay after school for one hour if they do not have a legitimate written excuse. The youth is frustrated because if she has to stay after school, she'll miss the school baseball game (FEELING/ANXIETIES). She makes several excuses, attempting to talk her way out of staying after school (NEGATIVE BEHAVIOR). The teacher tells the student to be quiet, accept the punishment, and begin her math assignment (OTHERS' REACTIONS creating more STRESS – Cycle 2 Begins). Becoming agitated (FEEL-INGS/ANXIETIES), the youth begins to yell at the teacher about being unfair (NEGATIVE BEHAV-IOR). The teacher responds by sarcastically saying, "You made your own bed, now you have to lie in it. You know the school policy" (OTHERS' REAC-TIONS creating more STRESS – Cycle 3 Begins). Embarrassed in front of her classmates (FEEL-INGS/ANXIETIES), the youth begins to scream and curse at the teacher (NEGATIVE BEHAVIOR). The teacher angrily yells at the youth to report to the office, which will result in a call home

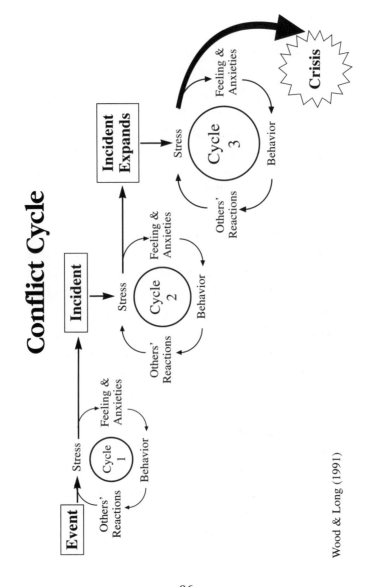

Conflict Cycle

Event → Stress → Cycle 1 → Feeling & Anxieties → Behavior → Others' Reactions

Incident → Stress → Cycle 2 → Feeling & Anxieties → Behavior → Others' Reactions

Incident Expands → Stress → Cycle 3 → Feeling & Anxieties → Behavior → Others' Reactions → Crisis

Wood & Long (1991)

(OTHERS' REACTIONS creating more STRESS – CRISIS). Now the youth is extremely frustrated over the additional consequence and knocks her books to the floor, throws a pen at the teacher, and tips over her desk before leaving the classroom and walking out of school.

It is easy to see why a coercive child's behavior develops the way it does. To change the child's behavior, the start of an interaction must be altered so that there are no harsh, aversive demands. Next, rather than giving in to the child's temper tantrums, the caregiver should deliver a consequence, such as loss of a privilege, to help the child learn the relationship between his or her behaviors and the consequences that follow. In the past, the coercive child was rewarded for negative behavior with control, dominance of others, and escape or avoidance from demands and unpleasant situations. Through the entire interaction, a caregiver must stay calm and not react with angry or negative behavior that will trigger more negative behavior from the youth. This stops the cycle of aversive behaviors and models self-control for the youth.

Teaching youth to use self-control strategies helps them begin to assume responsibility for changing their own antisocial behavior in ways that produce constructive and long-lasting results. If caregivers are successful in this task, kids will develop their skills to a point where they will no longer need to rely on adult authority for behavior control. They will have learned to manage their own behavior, control their impulses and feelings, live by rules and values, make constructive decisions rather than destructive decisions, and deal with others in their lives in a more positive manner.

References

Long, N.J., Morse, W.C., & Newman, R.G. (1996). **Conflict in the classroom.** Austin, TX: PRO-ED, Inc.

Long, N.J., & Wood, M.M. (1991). **Life space interaction.** Austin, TX: PRO-ED, Inc.

Patterson, G.R. (1982). **Coercive family process.** Eugene, OR: Castalia.

Crisis Teaching

"Crisis handled well can make positive, long-lasting changes; crisis managed ineptly will contribute to a devastating cycle of alienation, hostility, and aggression."

Long & Wood (1991)

John, 13, has just been admitted to his third school in four years. He was kicked out of his first school for skipping class, getting into fights with his classmates, and yelling at and arguing with his teachers. In the last school, John became so angry with a teacher, he pushed her over a chair. The situation isn't much different at home. John constantly complains and shouts at his mother when she asks him to help out or tells him something he doesn't want to hear. He also hits his little brother and sister when they play with his things without asking. Most of John's time is spent hanging out at the mall with his best friend, Terrence. Recently, John was kicked out of the mall for a month. A security guard was questioning John and Terrence about a shoplifting incident that neither boy was involved in. During the questioning, John suddenly snapped and began yelling at the guard, threatening to "kick his ass." Terrence had to hold John back so he wouldn't hit the guard. Since then, Terrence hasn't had anything to do with John because he is fed up with John's outbursts.

Many troubled kids like John make unhealthy choices when they lose self-control in times of conflict or crisis. While most people successfully deal with these conflict and crisis situations on a daily basis, kids who lack the key skills necessary to control their own behaviors during times of emotional distress many times respond with aggressive or negative behavior. This keeps them from successfully resolving conflicts, and leads to many negative consequences. In John's case, his inability to control himself negatively affects just about every part of his life. He has been through several schools and has been labeled a "belligerent" student. Teachers avoid John, and he doesn't get the academic help he needs. John's parents are extremely frustrated with his unwillingness to cooperate at home and school. Their relationship with John has soured as they've grown weary of the constant confrontations. Finally, John has few friends because of his explosive temper, and he just lost his one remaining companion.

How do we reach kids like John and help them learn the skills of self-control? At Boys Town, we've learned that the ability to control one's emotions and behaviors is a key to living a successful life. To teach the strategies children need in order to achieve this goal, Boys Town uses a method called Crisis Teaching. Kids who can face adverse situations without using negative or hurtful behaviors are more capable of getting their needs met, and are better able to cope with stress, positively change their behaviors, and successfully resolve conflicts. By using these self-control skills, kids are able to stop their usual negative responses, think of alternative ways of coping, and choose better ways of dealing with what can seem like insurmountable dilemmas. Children will inevitably face these situations time and again during their lives with parents, siblings, teachers, friends, and other adult authority figures. Teaching youth to use self-control strategies helps them begin to assume responsibility for changing their own antisocial behavior in ways that produce constructive and long-lasting results.

Simply put, self-control strategies are techniques that empower kids to calm themselves when they become upset. Eventually, children learn to use these strategies on their own as they become better at recognizing and anticipating events that cause them to lose self-control or become upset.

If caregivers are effective in teaching these skills, kids eventually will not have to rely on adult authority for behavior control. They will have learned to manage their own behavior, control their impulses and feelings, live by rules and values, make decisions that are constructive rather than destructive, and deal with others in a more positive manner.

Overview of Crisis Teaching

Through years of research and development, the Boys Town Teaching Model has evolved into a highly effective method of treatment for troubled kids. The Model has two main components: teaching skills and building relationships. Teaching skills to kids involves describing behavior and delivering consequences (positive and negative). Building a relationship with a child is essential if he or she is to learn and eventually use a skill consistently and correctly. These two components do not stand alone, but rather are dependent upon each other. When a child is taught a skill, a relationship is simultaneously being developed. For example, if a father takes his son fishing, he not only is teaching his son the skill of fishing, but also is strengthening their relationship by sharing an enjoyable experience.

This connection between teaching skills and building relationships spills over into many skill areas, including the skills that enable a child to maintain self-control. Let's look at the concepts and strategies that make up the process of Crisis Teaching, and how the Model's components serve as the foundation for this proven method of helping kids through a crisis.

Concepts of Crisis Teaching

Crisis Teaching comprises three central concepts – Staying Calm, De-escalating Behavior, and Cognitive Strategies. These concepts are incorporated into the Crisis Teaching process, which is presented in three phases. (These three phases will be explained in detail later in this article.)

Phase I emphasizes the concept of Staying Calm. This involves a set of steps designed to help the caregiver and child identify when the child is beginning to get upset and prevent the situation from escalating into a crisis. It also is critical for caregivers to remain calm and monitor their own behaviors. By remaining calm, caregivers can demonstrate self-control, which may help the child to calm down. This also allows caregivers to focus on their teaching, and avoid using words or actions that may cause the child's behaviors to worsen.

Phase II emphasizes the concept of De-escalating Behavior. Here, caregivers focus on helping the child to use a self-control strategy that has been taught beforehand. The child is given the opportunity to choose a strategy; if the child cannot or will not choose one, the caregiver chooses one for the child and guides the child toward using it. Once the child calms down, the caregiver moves to the next phase.

In Phase III, caregivers teach a calm child how to use self-control strategies when he or she becomes upset in the future. This addresses the concept of Cognitive Strategies. This teaching includes having the child earn negative consequences for losing self-control, and reviewing and practicing the strategy that can best help the child. The child earns positive consequences for practicing, which helps strengthen the caregiver-child relationship.

As you can see, there is an order and structure to the process of Crisis Teaching. However, this type of teaching also requires flexibility. Structure helps keep the teaching consistent and effective, and ensures that critical concepts are presented. Flexibility allows the person who is doing the teaching to modify the process to fit the child's needs and the circumstances of the situation. For example, you may have to use every step of Crisis Teaching with a child who is new to your program. On the other hand, you might shorten the process or use steps in a different order when teaching to a child whom you have been working with for some time, and who is familiar with your teaching style.

This flexibility also means that caregivers can use the same basic teaching method in a wide variety of programs and settings, with kids who have a wide range of problems. A good example would be a doctor who sees many different kinds of patients with various aliments. The doctor is trained and has many tools at his disposal. How he uses his training and tools is determined by the patient, the patient's symptoms, and how well the doctor knows the patient. With a patient who is visiting the doctor for the first time, the doctor might have to complete a comprehensive evaluation that requires questions about the person's ailment and medical history, a thorough examination, and many tests. The doctor will take his or her time and follow every step or procedure that is necessary. Once the patient's ailment is diagnosed, the doctor will prescribe treatment or a cure. However, if that patient comes in for treatment of the same ailment a number of times, the doctor won't have to go through a lengthy evaluation. He or she can simply check the patient's history and symptoms, make a diagnosis, and prescribe treatment.

The point here is that the better a caregiver gets to know a child, and identifies what tools work best with him or her, the more effective treatment the caregiver can provide. The structure of Crisis Teaching is always there, but the caregiver decides whether to use all or parts of the process. Ideally, the youth will begin to make the new learned behaviors part of his or her daily life and will know how to apply new skills to a variety of situations. The youth also is learning a different way of thinking and feeling because of the relationship-building and teaching that has occurred. The caregiver becomes more natural in his or her teaching, and can teach in a less-structured manner while still achieving the same positive results. Most importantly, the youth and the caregiver have benefited from their experience together.

Remember, Crisis Teaching is not meant to be a rigid, all-or-nothing teaching tool. Structure is essential, but decisions on how to teach to children on an individual basis must be made based on your experience and ability, the children you are working with, and the type of care you are providing.

Crisis Teaching can occur anytime. Children are constantly facing new situations that frustrate or anger them. By using these concepts, caregivers have a plan for effectively teaching self-control skills. That's how children learn and grow socially and emotionally.

Self-Control Strategies

Crisis Teaching incorporates individual, effective, and therapeutic strategies that can be used both in anticipation of a problem or during a crisis. These techniques (examples will be given later in the chapter) include cognitive and behavioral strategies, and can easily be taught in a variety of environments by adults who care for or work with kids – parents, teachers, and child-care professionals and caregivers who work in "out-of home" placements (e.g., shelters, foster care homes, mental health facilities, residential group homes).

Initially, you will steer an emotionally upset or angry youth through the calming process using cues, verbal prompts, and Corrective Teaching Interactions. (Corrective Teaching is a method that adults can use to address a child's negative or inappropriate behavior. It is discussed in detail in the article entitled, "Quality Teaching.") Ultimately, the goal is to have the child choose and correctly use a strategy after identifying circumstances that have led to emotional upheaval. When self-control strategies are used effectively, either with the help of adults or by the youth alone, crisis situations that could otherwise end up as destructive and belittling experiences instead become instructional and insightful.

In the remainder of this chapter we will discuss the elements, goals, and results of Crisis Teaching, including adult behaviors that make teaching more effective and specific self-control techniques that kids need. We also will discuss how to decide which strategies are right for kids, and the factors that affect these decisions. Finally, we'll look at how and why self-control strategies should be taught, and how teaching can be incorporated into different environments (e.g., home, classroom, more structured placements).

Quality Components For Effective Teaching

When using Crisis Teaching, it is important for you to realize that your behavior directly affects the way a child behaves. Depending upon how upset a child is and the severity of his or her behavior, you also may begin to feel upset, frustrated, or angry. These emotional responses can interfere with your ability to deal with the child's loss of self-control. If you become upset, it makes the child more upset and makes it more difficult to do constructive teaching. That's why it is essential that you remain as calm as possible.

It isn't always easy to stay calm when teaching. If a child is yelling, making threats, calling you or your loved ones names, or refusing to comply with instructions, you may initially respond emotionally rather than focusing on teaching to the youth's problem behaviors. If the goal of teaching during a crisis situation is for a child to learn self-control, it is essential for you to model self-control. The following sections explain some of the important physical and emotional elements – what we call quality components – that must be present when you work with children who have lost self-control. These quality components also should be present when you are doing other kinds of teaching.

Offer the youth "cool-down" time.
Offering kids a chance to cool down is an excellent
strategy for successfully managing a crisis. This
time is invaluable for you and the child. It is an
opportunity for you to regain your composure while
the youngster uses self-control strategies to calm
down. We will discuss this process later in the
chapter. (See the next section, "How to Use Crisis
Teaching.")

Kids also can be given time to cool down at
other times when they are upset or frustrated, not
just when they are in a crisis. Oftentimes, if a child
has an opportunity to cool down right away, a crisis
situation can be avoided. Otherwise, what starts as
a small problem can become bigger and bigger, just
like a snowball rolling down a hill. The child's ability to use a self-control strategy helps him or her to
put a stop to negative thoughts, and gives the child
something positive to work on.

**Spend more time telling the child what he
or she is doing right.** When a crisis occurs, adults
tend to focus on what a child is doing wrong. It is
easy to deal with these negative behaviors because
they are visible, obvious, and sometimes "in your
face." Examples of statements that are commonly
made to describe a child's inappropriate behavior
include: "You need to change your attitude"; "Quit

acting like a baby"; "Straighten up your act"; or "You're being a jerk." Besides being negative, these statements are extremely vague. With these types of unclear descriptions of inappropriate behaviors, the child has no idea what he or she should correct. Therefore, it's important to use descriptions that are understandable and specific. For example, statements like, "You are yelling and arguing," "Please stop pacing," or "You are glaring at me," let the child know exactly what he or she is doing. Keep in mind that if you spend too much time describing only inappropriate behavior, the child will see you as nagging, which could cause him or her to become more upset.

Focusing on a child's positive behaviors is difficult during a crisis situation. It doesn't seem natural. Positive behaviors are not as apparent, and your adrenaline is pumping, possibly causing you to become emotional. However, looking for positive behaviors is a good way to divert your attention away from the negative emotions you may be feeling. This can help you stay calm, and give you something positive to say to the youth, which will help him or her calm down, too.

To describe a child's appropriate behavior, use specific statements like, "Nice job of lowering your voice"; "You made a great decision to stop pacing and sit down"; "Thanks for looking at me so calmly and not glaring"; or "I really like the way you chose to start listening." Spending more time telling the youth what he or she is doing right will have a tremendous effect on your outlook during this stressful time. It will help you remain upbeat, positive, and calm.

Talk more softly and slowly. Think about how you feel when you are upset, frustrated, or nervous. When you begin to experience these uncomfortable emotions, things seem to speed up – thoughts start flying around in your head, you talk faster, your heartbeat quickens, and your voice gets louder. These all are normal physical responses to stressful emotions or feelings. Recognizing that they will happen in stressful situations helps you concentrate on controlling these behaviors.

The tone and volume of your voice can have a big impact on how a child in crisis responds to you. Talking loudly or shouting can make a child think that you are yelling at him or her, while talking fast only confuses the youth. This is a bad combination and will surely escalate a crisis situation. As you concentrate on lowering your voice and talking more slowly, you begin to calm yourself down. When you sound calm, you model how you want the child to speak. This is a big step toward averting or handling a crisis situation much more quickly because such modeling can soften the intensity of a child's inappropriate behaviors and head off further escalation.

Remain relaxed physically. Be aware of behaviors like clenching your fists, glaring at the child, pounding your hand on the table, towering over a kid, crossing your arms, and so on. A youth will perceive these kinds of actions as aggressive or threatening, and it will only make the situation worse. One excellent method for calming yourself physically is to take a deep breath, and let the air out slowly. Do this several times. This is an easy relaxation procedure that can be done quickly and almost anywhere. Your body will become less tense, and you will regain your composure.

Avoid arguing. In a crisis, some kids are masters at dragging adults into arguments and debates about issues that have nothing to do with the problem at hand. Their goal is to move away from the issue so that you will forget about the current difficulties they are having and the negative consequences they will earn. The next thing you know, you are debating whether or not the consequence a child earned two weeks ago was fair, or defending yourself against accusations that you don't really like the child.

113

Usually, this is a smoke screen that has helped the youth stay out of trouble in the past. The point is that when you get caught up in these trivial arguments and debates, you'll not only lose, but also become more frustrated and angry.

In these situations, you can keep your cool by letting the child know that you understand that he or she has some issues to discuss, and that you would be willing to discuss them once the child has calmed down and worked through the present problem. In this way, you demonstrate that you respect what the youth has to say, and you remain calm while avoiding a fruitless debate.

Avoiding these debates is a good rule of thumb. But, like any rule, there are exceptions. There will be times when immediately listening to what a child has to say can help solve a crisis. If a kid uncharacteristically becomes teary-eyed and begins sobbing, it is a good idea to ask what is wrong. It may be something you're not aware of – perhaps the child just got a disappointing phone call from a parent, caseworker, or friend. By asking what is wrong and being supportive, you may gain a better understanding of why the child is upset and the reason for the negative behaviors. You also are showing genuine concern, which goes a long way in strengthening your relationship with the child.

This is an excellent opportunity to spend some time talking through the problem with the child, and helping him or her find a solution. Later, once the intense emotions have subsided, you can return to the original issue and teach the youth a better way to deal with a problem.

A word of caution: Some kids learn to automatically turn on the tears at the first sign of trouble. Again, it is a behavior that may have allowed them to escape negative consequences in the past. When deciding whether to discuss an issue during a crisis situation, you will have to rely on your expertise and judgment. There is no tried-and-true formula to tell you when it is right or wrong. The key is to know the youth you are working with and to be sure that the behavior is one you don't normally see from that youth.

Watch your words. Don't say things that "put down" kids. Comments such as, "You'll never learn anything!"; "We've gone over this a thousand times!"; and "Are you stupid?" serve only to escalate a crisis and ruin relationships. Also, the manner in which you speak can send the child the message that you are putting him or her down. When you use a condescending or smug voice, even a positive statement like, "I think you're finally getting it," will be interpreted as phony and an insult. Treat each child respectfully, and accept the fact that some kids will need a lot more teaching than others before they begin to competently use skills on their own.

Another behavior that must be avoided at all times when teaching to kids is cursing. This is more likely to happen, intentionally or unintentionally, during the stressful and frustrating times when kids lose self-control. Throughout these intense situations, monitor your frustration level and be aware of what you are saying. Cursing or swearing is extremely unprofessional and poor modeling, and it also is a sure-fire way of intensifying a child's inappropriate behavior and badly damaging relationships. Always keep in mind the old saying: "You can catch more flies with honey than with vinegar." In other words, by treating kids with kindness, they are more likely to treat you with the same respect and kindness, even when they are upset.

Be careful not to use commands or statements like, "You need to quit arguing"; "Sit down right now"; "I want you to get off your bed"; or "You'd better start listening to me." These statements irritate kids and further escalate their behaviors. As the child becomes more and more upset, you may start to lose your temper.

116

Using "softer" words when making a request or giving a child an instruction allows you to remain calm and helps to keep the child's negative behavior from escalating. Softer, more soothing ways of saying the commands in the last paragraph are, "Would you please stop talking?"; "A better choice would be to sit down"; "Can you please get off your bed?"; and "It would be a good decision to look at me so I know you are listening." Here, you are sending the identical message, but in a more gentle way. Making requests in this type of calm, cool, and collected manner increases the chances that a child will comply and successfully work through a crisis.

Use statements of empathy, understanding, and concern. It is extremely hard for anyone – even adults – to calm down when they are angry or frustrated. Expecting kids to calm down quickly is unrealistic and demanding. Showing empathy and concern for an emotionally upset child helps defuse the highly charged emotions that can erupt during a crisis. Statements like, "I know it's really hard to pull yourself together when you're upset," or "You are really upset, and I want to help you work through this so you can feel better," let the youth know that you understand what they are experiencing and are concerned about their wellbeing. Statements of concern and understanding are

117

extremely effective in helping you and the child calm down.

Empathy statements work best with children who have a strong relationship with a caregiver. This doesn't mean that adults shouldn't use empathy with a child they don't know very well. But when these statements are overused or sound phony, especially in situations where the caregivers and the child are still trying to establish a trusting relationship, it only serves to make the youth more upset. You don't appear genuine, and the kids know it! For some kids, the use of empathy and concern won't help to calm them down. When you hear responses from kids such as, "You don't know how I feel!" or "You don't really care about me!", it means you are grating on the child's nerves and should stop using these statements. However, this may be an opportunity to use a concern statement like, "I don't know exactly how you are feeling, but I want to help you." Also, it may be more effective to use empathy when a child is depressed, sad, or lonely than when a child is angry or aggressive.

Use positive correction. At some time during your teaching, you will give a negative consequence for a child's negative behavior. This usually involves taking away all or part of a privilege or something else the child likes. Many times when this happens, kids don't see any light at the end of the tunnel and focus solely on what they just lost as a consequence. That is why it is important to tell kids they will have a chance to earn back some of the consequence by practicing behaviors that you want to see. We call this a positive correction statement, and it gives kids a ray of hope. It may be just what they need to hear in order to begin to calm down. An example might be, "Mary, remember that you will have a chance to earn back some of the TV time you lost when you calm down and start working this out."

It does no good to continually remind a child of the consequence that was given. This may only make the child more agitated. Use positive correction when the opportunity presents itself. For example, a child may have just complained about a consequence. This would be a perfect time to tell the youth that he or she can earn some of the consequence back by using positive behaviors.

Use positive correction selectively. A good rule of thumb is to not let a child earn back more than half of the consequence. For example, if a youngster earned a consequence of losing one hour of TV time, then the most he or she could earn back would be a half hour of TV time. How much a child earns back depends on how serious the behavior was, how long it took the child to cool down, and how well he or she practiced the appropriate skill. Of course, less of the consequence can be earned back when a child's behaviors are more intense, more serious, last a long time, or if the child half-heartedly participates in the practice. On the other hand, if the child's behaviors are not as serious as they have been, or if he or she calms down more quickly or actively engages in the practice session, then giving back half of the consequence can really get the child's attention. The message you are sending is, "The sooner you pull yourself together, the smaller the consequence will be."

Know your child. Every child has unique needs, and the way you teach will vary accordingly. Many variables must be considered when implementing the steps of Crisis Teaching. As discussed earlier, this is not a rigid process, but a natural series of behaviors and responses to those behaviors. Its success relies on your ability to know your child, and to determine which components to use, and when and how to use them.

One of the most important variables is your relationship with a child. When there is a positive relationship, a child is much more likely to listen to you, want to please you, and follow your instructions. Thus, a child is more likely to learn how to control his or her behavior in a crisis situation, and to retain and use the skills you are teaching. In a healthy relationship, caregivers can use such qualities as humor, nicknames, or shared experiences in their teaching. These same qualities, when used by a caregiver who does not have a strong relationship with a youth, may be perceived as sarcastic, condescending, or meaningless.

A factor in healthy relationships is for caregivers to understand that after a crisis situation is over, it's over. In other words, caregivers must not hold a grudge against youth for their negative behaviors. Even though a youth may have used nasty or hurtful words, you must treat what the youth said or did as behaviors and not as personal attacks. This isn't easy to do. But it is very effective in building a solid relationship, one where a child's past negative behavior will not be dredged up as a constant reminder that he or she made bad choices. Kids need support in crisis situations, not a verbal replay of the mistakes they've made.

Other important variables are a child's age and developmental level. With an older child, you may be able to use logic. Some older children respond to teaching that explains the effect their behavior has on others. With younger children, you may have to be firmer, use simpler words, and make the teaching process shorter. That's because these kids usually have a shorter attention span, or will use certain behaviors in order to receive attention of any kind. Young children or children at a lower developmental level may not be able to learn skills as quickly and may need repeated interactions.

Any physical, emotional, or intellectual disability that a child may have also affects how you teach. You may have to simplify your teaching, use shorter words and sentences, demonstrate or model certain behaviors, or spend more time teaching.

The length of time a caregiver knows a child also plays a role in effective teaching. Obviously, parents will have known their children all their lives. But in settings where caregivers work with new children all the time, how long they've known a child usually will determine how much and what kind of teaching occurs. Under most circumstances, it may be necessary to use Crisis Teaching more often with children who are new to a program. On the other hand, the longer a child has been in a program and the more opportunities you have had to teach him or her, the fewer times you should have to use Crisis Teaching.

Finally, the number of children you have to work with greatly affects the time you can spend with each child. Logically, the fewer kids you are caring for – whether you are a parent or a caregiver – the more opportunities for teaching you will have with each youth. This can lead to fewer situations where children lose self-control. If you are responsible for a large group of kids, you will have fewer opportunities to teach to each child. This could result in more situations where children lose self-control. Therefore, it is best to have an adult-to-child ratio that is as low as possible.

All of these factors have an impact on the way you implement Crisis Teaching. It is imperative that you get to know each child you work with as well as you can.

Teaching kids skills and self-control techniques is an interactive process. If you aren't careful, some kids may try to manipulate you and "teach" you to use inappropriate behaviors. It is important to always be aware of your own behaviors, especially during times when you may become upset. Unless you are in control of yourself, it is impossible to teach a child how to maintain self-control. When you remain calm, the kids have the time they need to calm down and think about the self-control strategies they want to use. The goal should not be to control children, but to teach them how to exercise self-control.

How to Use Crisis Teaching

Despite your best efforts to build on a child's strengths and prevent problem behaviors, there will be times when a child will engage in behaviors that are subtly or overtly disruptive. When these inappropriate behaviors continue and interfere with your teaching, they are called "ongoing behaviors." Ongoing behaviors can range from passivity, withdrawal, and silence to arguing, complaining, swearing, laughing, or not following instructions. It also may include making threats, damaging property, or physical aggression.

Despite the variety of ongoing behaviors, there is a common element that indicates the need for Crisis Teaching – the youngster is no longer following your instructions. Regardless of the severity or intensity of the behaviors, the same basic process can be used to help the youth regain self-control.

Below is a list of each of the phases and concepts, along with the suggested steps, that give structure to the Crisis Teaching process. An explanation of each follows.

- Phase I – Staying Calm
- Phase II – De-escalating Behavior
- Phase III – Cognitive Strategies

Phase I – Staying Calm

Staying Calm has two goals: to prevent extreme emotional outbursts (when possible), and to help children quickly recognize and stop such outbursts when they do occur. In other words, the youth is given a chance to stop the negative behavior before it becomes so serious that worse things happen. The key to this phase is the caregiver's ability to shape and direct the child's behavior toward calming down.

Phase I – Staying Calm Steps

- Corrective Teaching begins (first consequence delivered).

- When ongoing behavior occurs, give the youth an instruction with a statement of understanding.

- If ongoing behavior continues, use the four ongoing tools:

    1. Give statements of understanding.

    2. Describe what was done wrong, and describe what to do right.

3. Praise improvements in behavior.

4. Give reality statements.

(If you switch from one tool to another, pause and give the youth a chance to calm down.)

• If ongoing behavior continues, deliver a second consequence for losing self-control. (This consequence is predetermined.)

• Offer the youth a chance to work through the problem. Include a positive correction statement.

(If the youth agrees to calm down and begins to demonstrate self-control at this time, then return to the original issue. If the youth continues to engage in ongoing behavior, move to Phase II – De-escalating Behavior.)

Situations where kids lose self-control may be preventable in part because the antecedent conditions are fairly predictable. Frequently, many children lose self-control when they have been corrected or have been told something they did not want to hear, such as a "No" answer. The youth also may have difficulty accepting criticism, accepting a consequence, or even following instructions. Every kid will lose self-control for different reasons, and one of the key elements to a child learning how to maintain self-control is his or her ability to learn and correctly use these other skills. So, it is important for caregivers to identify what skill deficiencies are causing the child problems, and focus and target their everyday teaching on helping the child learn and internalize these more basic skills. When children learn and use these skills competently, Crisis Teaching becomes unnecessary.

Over time, caregivers learn to identify cues in a youth's behavior that may lead to teaching situations. They also will learn what behaviors indicate that a child is losing self-control (e.g., short, sharp answers, tight muscles, lack of acknowledgment, and so on). Once these are identified, staff should teach kids to recognize the triggers that precede a loss of self-control. If children are eventually able to correctly and consistently identify what behaviors lead to a loss of self-control, they will be better equipped to head-off a crisis on their own.

Occasionally, a youth may have a series of difficult experiences that you didn't observe or know about (e.g., problems with a friend at school). If these problems frustrate or anger the child, it is possible that a routine interaction with you may cause the child to lose self-control.

In these situations, one general key to successfully avoiding a crisis is recognizing early that a youth is having problems and taking a preventive approach to deal with the youth's behaviors. At the first sign that a child's behaviors are becoming inappropriate, you must decide what method of intervention to use. Normally, you would begin by saying something like, "It appears that something is bothering you. If you sit down and calmly talk about the problem, I'd be willing to discuss it with you." This gives the youngster an opportunity to calm down and explain the problem.

Many children do not have the skills they need to deal with certain emotional situations; therefore, you may opt to use a problem-solving or counseling approach if it appears that a youth is displaying uncharacteristic behaviors. For example, if a youth who normally handles most situations calmly reacts to a routine instruction with an emotional response, then counseling may be necessary. In these cases, by choosing counseling instead of Corrective Teaching, you may prevent an interaction that could damage relationships or escalate the youth's negative behavior. Discretion and good judgment are key elements in knowing which approach to take. However, in most situations where a child is upset, you should use Crisis

Teaching to calm the child and maintain an appropriate tolerance.

If the child continues his or her ongoing behavior and will not discuss the situation calmly, begin Corrective Teaching. During this teaching, the child earns a consequence for the original inappropriate behavior. If the child continues the ongoing behavior, you can give a simple, firm instruction (e.g., "Right now you are talking. Please stop talking."), or a statement of understanding to calm the youth (e.g., "I understand it's hard to listen to criticism. Please sit down and stop yelling. I do want to listen to what you have to say."). If the child responds by following your instruction, you should generously praise him or her and decide whether it is necessary to continue the Crisis Teaching process. If the child is able to follow instructions and accept his or her consequences at this time, you should complete the Corrective Teaching Interaction.

(Note: If at any time during Phase I, the child regains self-control and stops the ongoing behaviors, it is not necessary to continue to the next step of Phase I. Complete your Corrective Teaching on the original issue, and follow up on any positive correction statement you've made.)

If the child continues to engage in negative behaviors, you can use the four "tools" to de-escalate ongoing behavior. The four tools are: 1) Statements of understanding (e.g., "I know you're upset right now."); 2) Descriptions of what was done wrong, and what to do right (e.g., "You're pacing; please sit down."); 3) Praise for improvements in behavior (e.g., "You've stopped yelling; nice job."); and 4) Reality statements (e.g., "The sooner you start working with me, the sooner you can start doing some things you like doing."). When used skillfully by a caregiver, these four tools are extremely effective in helping an upset child to regain self-control. Keep in mind that it is important to use all of these tools; that is, if one isn't working, try another. If you move from one tool to another, do so slowly, and continue to give the child a chance to calm down.

The time you spend using the four tools will vary from child to child, and will depend on the intensity or severity of the child's behavior. If the child's inappropriate behavior increases in intensity and severity during this time, you will move to the De-escalating Behavior (Phase II) more quickly. But if a child is responding to any of the four tools, you should continue to use them until the child calms down. If this happens, complete Corrective Teaching.

A word of caution is necessary here. As we mentioned earlier, it is important during teaching to focus on the child's appropriate behavior as much as possible. Since one of the four tools calls for describing what the child is doing wrong during your teaching, this tool should be used selectively. Even though it is important for the child to understand what he or she is doing wrong, frequently bringing up these behaviors can only serve to fuel the fire. The youth will view you as nagging, punishing, or belittling, and will be less likely to listen to what you are saying. The goal of any caregiver should be to focus as much as possible on positive behaviors and to use praise whenever a child is displaying improvements in behavior. This takes a great deal of patience, ability to observe and describe situations, and self-control on the part of the caregiver.

If the child's inappropriate behaviors continue or escalate, you may need to deliver a second consequence, this time for not maintaining self-control. When the consequence is given, it should be paired with a positive correction statement (e.g., "I know this is hard for you. Right now you're not showing self-control and have earned a consequence. But you can earn some of the consequence back if you calm down and start working with me.").

The child's age and developmental level will determine how quickly you give this consequence. For younger children or those at a lower developmental level, you may give the consequence quickly because they have a shorter attention span, and many times the sole purpose of their behaviors is to get attention. With older children or those at a higher developmental level, you may wait so they have an opportunity to start regaining self-control. If they continue the inappropriate behavior after a reasonable time, give the second consequence.

The final step in the Staying Calm Phase is to offer the child one last chance to work through the issue. You might say, "You can begin making good choices right now and work with me. Are you able to do this now?" If the child answers "Yes," you should again tell the child how you expect him or her to behave while you first discuss the original issue and the child's loss of self-control. If the child responds appropriately, generously praise him or her for regaining control, and return to teaching on the original issue. At that point, the child can earn back half of each of the two consequences – the first positive correction is for calmly discussing loss of self-control, and the second is for appropriately returning to the original issue. On the other hand, if the child does not respond appropriately, or continues to escalate an inappropriate behavior, then it is time to move directly to the De-escalating Behavior Phase.

Phase II – De-escalating Behavior

During this phase, you will work with the child until he or she begins to regain self-control. A child can earn a final consequence, but it is not given until Phase III – Cognitive Strategies.

Phase II – De-escalating Behavior Steps

- Ask the youth to select a self-control strategy; if the youth cannot or will not, select a strategy for the child. (For self-control strategies, see pages 134-135.)

- Use the four ongoing tools and the self-control strategy to help the youth regain self-control. (Give statements of understanding, describe what was done wrong and describe what to do right, praise improvements in behavior, and give reality statements.)

- Test for self-control with two simple instructions.

Self-Control Strategies

Deep-breathing

- Take a deep breath in through your nose and hold it for about two seconds.
- Let the breath out slowly through your mouth.
- Repeat this process two or three times until you feel yourself calming down.
- When you are calm, tell an adult.

Journaling or drawing

- Go to a designated place where you won't be disturbed.
- Write down (or draw a picture showing) how you are feeling and what you're thinking.
- When you are calm, tell an adult.

Take time to cool down

- Go to a designated place where you won't be disturbed or distracted.
- Take an agreed-on amount of time to calm down.
- If you need more time, calmly ask for it.
- When you are calm, tell an adult.

Positive self-talk

- Make a positive comment about how you can handle a situation appropriately. Use a phrase like, "I can get myself under control"; "I've done it before, I can do it again"; "If I stop now, things will get better"; or "I can do this."

- Repeat the statement you choose until you are calm.

- When you are calm, tell an adult.

Muscle relaxation

- Clench and squeeze your fists for five seconds, and slowly release them.

- Slowly roll your neck in circles for five seconds.

- Scrunch your shoulders and slowly roll them in circles several times.

- Slowly rotate your ankles.

- Raise your eyebrows as high as you can and slowly lower them.

- Scrunch your face, and release.

- When you are calm, tell an adult.

- Review behaviors that demonstrate self-control (e.g., calm voice, eye contact, sitting up straight, answering questions, etc.).

Upon entering the De-escalating Behavior Phase, ask the child to choose a self-control strategy that he or she has learned (e.g., deep-breathing, muscle relaxation, journaling, positive self-talk, taking time to cool down).

If the youngster is unable or unwilling to choose a strategy, then you should choose one. If this happens, the youth earns a negative consequence, given later, for not choosing a self-control strategy. If the child chooses a strategy, he or she earns a positive consequence, which also is given later. The goal is to teach the child that it is better for him or her to choose a self-control strategy than for you to select one for the child.

As we mentioned earlier, it is important to stay calm, talk in a nonthreatening voice, and talk slowly. Controlling your emotions is the single most important factor during this phase. Throughout the De-escalating Behavior Phase, you should continue to offer statements of understanding, and praise the child for any improvements in behavior as he or she begins to calm down (e.g., "Good; you stopped yelling. I know it's hard to stay calm when you're upset."). Positive correction statements let the youngsters know that by calming down and following instructions, they are on the right path to regaining self-control.

Describing what the child is doing wrong and what he or she should be doing right also helps guide the child back to self-control (e.g., "You're walking around. Please sit down so we can talk."). When dealing with any ongoing inappropriate behavior, your instructions first should focus on the more overt behaviors, such as walking around, yelling, slamming doors, etc. (Again, use discretion here so that you don't continually repeat what the child is doing wrong.)

As De-escalating Behavior continues, the youth's behavior is likely to de-escalate and escalate several times. The goals are to reduce the number of times negative behavior escalates, decrease the length of time a child is in crisis, and increase the number of times the youth's behavior improves.

In addition to offering statements of understanding, describing correct behavior, and praising improvements, there are several other important factors to remember as you help the child resolve the situation. First, the youth may complain about the negative consequence he or she was given; you

137

can respond with a statement of understanding and show that you are willing to help the child earn back some of the consequence (e.g. "I know you've lost something important. I'd like to help you earn some of the consequence back.").

During this phase, it is not necessary to continually talk to the youngster. If you respond to every comment the youth makes and try to fill in uncomfortable pauses or give too many instructions, he or she may view this as badgering. As we mentioned earlier, this may escalate, rather than reduce, the youth's inappropriate behavior. Also, any statement of praise or understanding must be sincere or it could further provoke the child. Use brief, easily understood statements and appropriate pauses.

The youth also may want to argue with you and set up a power struggle, or make demands (e.g., "I have the right to call my probation officer.") or accusations (e.g., "You're not fair to me!"). Don't be drawn into arguments or discussions of outside issues. Your primary task is to help the child regain self-control, and you must stay focused on that task. The best way to handle demands, accusations, and arguing behavior is to offer understanding statements and indicate a willingness to discuss the issue or consider a request after the youngster has calmed down. You then can redirect the youth to the task at hand (e.g., "You can make that phone call after you calm down," or "I know you're upset, and I want to talk about fairness, but right now please...."). By focusing on the problem, you can avoid side issues that will only prolong the child's loss of self-control and disrupt the teaching process.

As you work through the crisis, stay reasonably close to the child. You should be close enough to talk, but not so close that you invade his or her private space; this could cause the child to strike out at you. In general, stay at least an arm's length away. If the youngster is walking around or leaves the room, you should stay nearby, but don't "stalk" him or her by following too closely. If the youth is pacing around a room, simply stand in a strategic location or move a few feet one way or the other to stay reasonably close.

Again, it is important that you control your emotions and behaviors when a youth loses self-control. The child may engage in many behaviors that are aimed at getting you angry or involved in content, side issues, or discussions about whether you care about him or her. The child may act aggressively defiant in an attempt to get you to stop teaching and leave. Or he or she may act passively defiant to make you upset. In all of these situations, the youth is trying to control your behavior. The key to preventing this is consistent use of Crisis Teaching, varying the procedures to fit the youth's behavior. Once you find something that helps the child calm down, go ahead and use it!

Caregivers should keep these tips in mind:

1. Remain calm.

2. Don't try to "out talk" or talk louder than the youth; wait for the child to quiet down for a few seconds before speaking.

3. Don't respond to the youth's allegations about fairness; the issue is the child's current behavior, not your actions.

4. Don't be afraid of short silences; however, don't let the silences run too long.

5. It is important to give children the time and space they need to calm down. This is accomplished by having the child choose and correctly use a self-control strategy.

The De-escalating Behavior Phase can last anywhere from several minutes to several hours or longer, but the youth eventually will begin to make some progress toward calming down. Once you think the youth is ready to work with you, you then can test whether he or she is calming down by giving simple instructions. Be careful not to give too many instructions (two should be enough) or instructions that could provoke more negative behavior. Before any teaching can be done, the youngster must be able to follow the steps of following instructions – looking at you, acknowledging what you are say, doing the task, and checking back.

Once the child is able to follow instructions appropriately and appears to have regained self-control, review and practice behaviors that demonstrate self-control. For example, you may tell the child that he or she should use a calm voice, look at you, sit up straight, and answer questions. These behaviors will demonstrate that the child has regained self-control and is now ready for teaching. This completes the De-escalating Behavior Phase.

Phase III – Cognitive Strategies

Phase III begins when the youngster is able to follow instructions and is not using inappropriate behaviors. In the early steps of this phase, you should continue to praise and specifically describe any appropriate behavior.

Once you feel that the youth is calm and can follow instructions, Phase III occurs. Because one goal of this phase is to get the youth to accept the consequences he or she has earned, remind the youth of the steps of that skill. If the youth does not appear completely ready to accept the real consequences, you may choose to have him or her practice accepting consequences in a pretend situation. When the youth is ready, give the consequences. Praising the child for appropriate behaviors at this time is very critical (e.g., "You're doing a super job of looking at me and nodding your head.").

(Note: If you had to select the self-control strategy for the youth, then more teaching needs to be done to improve the youth's ability to choose a calming skill when in crisis. In addition to the child earning a negative consequence, a complete review and practice of a self-control strategy is necessary. If the youth chose a self-control strategy, he or she receives a positive consequence, and no review or practice is necessary.)

Next, you should praise the child for remaining calm and following instructions during this phase. Specifically describe the behaviors the child is currently engaging in that demonstrate self-control (e.g., remaining seated and quiet, looking at you, using a pleasant voice tone, and so on) and give the child a positive consequence for those behaviors.

The final step of this phase is to complete Corrective Teaching on the original issue.

Phase III – Cognitive Strategies Steps

- Prompt how to accept consequences (or practice).

- Review the consequences the youth earned; if the youth is ready, give him or her the consequences. The consequences are as follows:

  1. The child earns a negative consequence if the caregiver had to choose a self-control strategy; a review and practice of the self-control strategy is necessary.

     OR

  2. The child earns a positive consequence if he or she chose the self-control strategy; a review and practice of the self-control strategy is not necessary.

- The child earns a positive consequence for the behaviors he or she is currently using that demonstrate self-control.

- Return to the original issue, and begin a Corrective Teaching Interaction.

143

Developing Individual Self-Control Strategy Plans

It is extremely important to choose the right self-control strategies for kids who are not able to successfully handle anger, frustration, conflict, and crisis. These strategies should meet each youth's individual needs, and suit him or her best in times of crisis. As you consider the strategies that have been described, these factors should serve as guidelines for matching techniques with the needs of each child:

Age and developmental level. Some self-control strategies are geared for and are more suited to older youth, while other strategies are more appropriate for younger children. For example, drawing would be a better strategy than writing in a journal for a younger child who has not yet learned to write or a youth who is unable to express himself through writing. In these cases, choosing the wrong strategies can actually lead to a crisis situation because the child's inability to perform them leads to frustration. Strategies such as drawing, deep-breathing, and taking time to calm down that divert the child's attention away from the crisis situation are most effective with younger or developmentally handicapped children.

144

Severity of behaviors. Many troubled youth have behavior problems that are quite severe. Problems related to the safety of the child and others may initially require the use of self-control strategies that are appropriate for a situation, simple to teach, and easy for the youth to use anywhere. For example, if a girl who has a history of hurting herself and being aggressive toward others is facing a crisis situation, giving her a pen to write in a journal could create an extremely dangerous situation. Instead, calming techniques like deep-breathing, muscle relaxation, or positive self-talk would work better and be safer.

Exposure to teaching. The length of time you have been working with a youth on teaching self-control issues also will play a role in determining appropriate strategies. A child who has been working on this problem area for some time and has been making progress in using calming techniques may be ready to learn more advanced strategies. With these kids, calming strategies such as writing in a journal, progressive muscle relaxation, positive self-talk, anger logs, hassle logs, and others may be extremely effective and therapeutic. On the other hand, children who are new to this approach would be taught more basic calming techniques.

As a youth gets better at using self-control strategies, you can begin to teach new strategies. For example, a child may progress from going to his bedroom to draw in a notebook when he gets upset at home, to writing in a journal at the kitchen table, to using deep-breathing in any situation where he experiences frustration or anger. This is a process that usually develops and improves slowly over time, so be patient. Keep in mind that the final goal is to teach children to choose and correctly use a self-control strategy on their own when stressful feelings begin to overwhelm them.

Setting. Some settings in a child's life are more suitable for using specific self-control strategies than others. For example, a child may use the self-control strategy of drawing in his room at home. However, this may not be an appropriate strategy to use in a setting outside the home. That's why it is important for children to learn a number of self-control strategies that can be used in different settings (e.g., school, sports, church, work, etc.).

Child's response. This factor involves a child's willingness to learn and use a particular self-control strategy, and its observed effectiveness. It is fruitless to try to teach a strategy that a youth does not want to use. In addition, if you observe that a child is not using a certain calming technique, then it is necessary to replace it with a different strategy. One of the best ways to prevent this from happening is to have the child involved in the process of identifying which strategies will be taught and used. This gives the child a sense of ownership and involvement, and makes it more likely that these strategies will be used in crisis situations.

Proactive Teaching and Self-Control

When kids are just starting to learn self-control strategies, you will spend a great deal of time doing what we call Proactive Teaching. Proactive Teaching is a teaching method that is used to anticipate and head off problems and crises before they happen. When you teach to problem areas before they occur, children are set up for success in situations where they have previously made poor choices. As a child starts using these newly learned skills and begins experiencing success, the child will view you as being helpful and concerned. This helps to further develop and enhance positive relationships. Proactive Teaching is a real key to the youth's success and to your sense of accomplishment.

Proactive Teaching can be used to teach youth basic and advanced social skills and self-control strategies, prepare youth for specific situations

147

or circumstances, and remedy specific skill deficiencies. This type of teaching can be done on an individual basis or with a group of youth, depending on the circumstances.

There are many opportunities for this type of teaching during the course of a day. As youth progress and begin to use their self-control strategies, you will spend less time doing Proactive Teaching and use more cues and verbal prompts instead. Eventually, kids will consistently and correctly use these calming strategies as they begin to successfully resolve conflicts on their own. However, achieving this goal can often be a slow, arduous, and frustrating process. You must remain patient and continue to make the most of your opportunities to teach preventively if you are to help youth learn new ways to control their behavior.

In the Boys Town Teaching Model, kids are assigned three self-control strategies. As we stated earlier, one strategy may work better than the others in certain settings and situations. Even though the youth have three calming strategies to use, you can preventively teach other strategies that may be better suited to specific environments.

General Proactive Teaching Guidelines

- Start your teaching session at a time when the youth is calm and not misbehaving. This is when a youth should be most receptive to your instruction.

- Identify a self-control strategy, and give examples of how and when it can be used.

- Specifically describe the appropriate steps of the strategy.

- Give rationales, or reasons, for using the strategy. These rationales are your selling points for why the youth should learn and use the skill. Here, you let the youth know what good things might happen when he or she chooses to use the calming skill.

- As you teach, ask the youth if he or she understands what you are saying.

- Have the youth practice using the strategy in a pretend situation. Give the youth feedback on the practice, and reinforce him or her for practicing.

When to Use Proactive Teaching With Self-Control Strategies

There are several ways to use Proactive Teaching in order to review and practice self-

149

control strategies. These various teaching opportunities are discussed here.

Empowerment Conference. This concept, which is part of the Boys Town Teaching Model, is a powerful Proactive Teaching opportunity. The conference involves having an adult and a youth sit down at a planned time every day to discuss, review, and practice self-control strategies, along with other pertinent social skills. Because this is a neutral time, and the process encourages and promotes active involvement, the youth is better able to pay attention and participate. Thus, the youth is more likely to learn because he or she is receptive to your teaching.

This scheduled Proactive Teaching opportunity can take place in almost any environment where kids are experiencing self-control problems (e.g., school, home, or out-of-home placement). You can review and practice different strategies each day so that the youth become proficient in all three of their targeted strategies.

The main emphasis of the Empowerment Conference is having the youth practice self-control strategies. This can include a discussion of the various situations and environments where the strategies can be used (e.g., home, school, with peers), which promotes learning how to use the strategies in different settings. A specific and thorough review, demonstration, and practice of the strategy follows. To promote better learning, come up with practice situations that are realistic to the youth and related to an area in which he or she is currently struggling (e.g., problems in the classroom or with a sibling at home). This daily repetition is a key ingredient to acquiring self-control skills. Using a daily Empowerment Conference enables you to do more teaching, which helps kids learn and ultimately master calming strategies.

Individual and group teaching. Since Proactive Teaching is so flexible, it can be used in both individual and group teaching sessions. This is especially helpful in settings where a number of youth are not using their calming strategies, even when you give cues and verbal prompts.

When teaching to one youth, you can spend more time reviewing and practicing calming techniques. Much like an Empowerment Conference, this additional teaching time can be invaluable in helping children learn to stop their inappropriate behaviors and successfully resolve conflicts.

Group teaching sessions enable you to teach to a larger number of kids in a short amount of time.

Most likely, youth will be at different stages of progress in their use of strategies. Kids who have been with you for a while and have successfully learned to use their strategies when they are upset are excellent role models for newer children who are struggling in this area. Devoting an entire group teaching session to reviewing and practicing skills is an effective way to provide extra teaching to youth who are experiencing difficulty.

Following a crisis. The time after a crisis situation in which a youth had trouble choosing a self-control strategy is an excellent Proactive Teaching opportunity. If a youth uses inappropriate behaviors instead of a self-control strategy, even when you have provided cues or prompts, talking about how using the strategy would have changed the outcome provides the child with a fantastic opportunity to learn from a real-life crisis. The youth is given an immediate opportunity to learn how to better handle a crisis situation in the future.

Family Meeting. Family Meeting (also called Community Meeting) is another unique teaching opportunity that is part of the Boys Town Teaching Model. Here, you can review and role-play self-control strategies with a group of young people.

Family Meeting is a time when all the kids get together to solve problems, practice skills, discuss other topics and activities, or make decisions. These meetings can be held in a home, a group or foster care home, a youth shelter, or any other youth-care setting.

Many calming techniques can be taught in this type of group setting (e.g., deep-breathing, progressive muscle relaxation, journaling or drawing, and so on). Dedicating an entire Family Meeting to having the kids review and practice one of these calming strategies is an effective and efficient way to reach more children.

"As needed." Whenever you observe youth consistently choose to use destructive behaviors instead of self-control strategies during crisis situations, Proactive Teaching is needed. Some troubled youth have these inappropriate responses to conflict deeply ingrained in their learning histories. Therefore, it will take many teaching sessions before they show even the slightest improvement. In these cases, it is a good idea at various times throughout the day to spontaneously review and practice a youth's self-control strategies.

Generalization and Self-Control Strategies

Generalization means that a person who learned to use a skill in one situation knows how to use the skill in different situations. This means that a self-control strategy does not have to be retaught in each new setting or situation in order for a child to know how to use it. In the Boys Town Teaching Model, the belief is that if children have learned calming skills, they can use them anywhere.

Generalization can be promoted by having the youth thoroughly review and practice targeted strategies under conditions that are as similar as possible to the real-life situations he or she may face. This way, they gain experience in dealing with real-life problems, issues, and events without having to worry about making mistakes or failing. This helps set them up for success in situations where they normally have problems maintaining self-control.

Using Crisis Teaching

Let's go back to John, our example at the beginning of the chapter. As you might recall, John has had difficulty maintaining self-control in a variety of environments. This has led to many negative consequences – being kicked out of two schools, poor relationships with his parents and siblings, serious conflicts with authority, and loss of friends. Now, John's inability to control his behaviors has led to court involvement and ultimately has resulted in him being placed into an out-of-home placement.

The following is an example of how Crisis Teaching might sound the first time a caregiver works with John when he loses self-control. Remember that John is new to the program, has not had many Crisis Teaching Interactions, and is unfamiliar with the caregiver's teaching style. Here, the caregiver will provide more structure to his or her teaching by incorporating all the steps to Crisis Teaching.

Phase I – Staying Calm

John: *"May I go to my room and listen to the radio?"*

Caregiver: *"John, thanks for asking permission so nicely. But we're getting ready for a group activity, so this time I'll have to say 'No.'"*

John: (stands up and shouts) *"I'm not going to go to any stupid group! It's my damn radio, and I'll listen to it any time I want to! You can't tell me what to do; you're not my parents!"*

155

- **Start Corrective Teaching**

  Caregiver: *"John, I understand it's hard for you to accept 'No' at times. Why don't you take a few deep breaths like we practiced so you can calm down."* (pause)

  John: (John begins to walk around the room and continues to yell) *"You are so damned unfair, I can't believe it!"*

  Caregiver: *"John, right now you are yelling and pacing around. You're not accepting 'No' for an answer and you've earned a consequence. You will be able to earn some of that consequence back when we practice that skill."*

  John: (continuing to yell and pace) *"Shut up, you idiot!"* (pause)

- **Give a simple instruction with a statement of understanding**

  Caregiver: *"John, I know you're frustrated. But you're walking around the room. Please sit down in the chair."*

  John: (angry voice tone and continued pacing) *"I can never do anything! I hate you!"*

Ongoing behavior – use four tools.

● **Give a statement of understanding**

Caregiver: *"I understand you're upset and that you really want to listen to your radio."*

John: (shouting) *"You don't know anything about how I feel! Leave me alone!"*

Caregiver: (pause)

● **Describe what was done wrong, and describe what to do right**

Caregiver: *"John, right now you're shouting. A better choice is to lower your voice."*

John: (in a louder voice tone) *"This really sucks! I hate it here!"*

Caregiver: (pause)

● **Praise improvements in behavior**

John: (continues to walk around, but is no longer talking)

Caregiver: *"Thanks for quieting down, John."*

John: (yelling in angry voice tone) *"Will you shut up! I'm not going to do anything you tell me, so leave me alone! All I want to do is listen to my damn radio!"*

Caregiver: (pause)

● Give a reality statement

Caregiver: *"John, the sooner you begin following instructions and calm down, the more quickly you can start doing some things you like to do."*

John: (angrily yelling and pacing) *"I'm sick and tired of this shit! I can't believe how unfairly you treat me."*

Caregiver: (pause)

● Give a statement of understanding

Caregiver: *"I know it's hard to follow instructions right now, but it is the only way we are going to get this problem solved."*

John: (still shouting and pacing) *"Are you deaf? I said I'm not going to follow any instructions!"*

Caregiver: (pause)

John: (yelling and moving closer to caregiver) *"I ain't doin' nothin' and you can't make me!"*

Caregiver: (pause)

John: (continues to pace and yell)

● **Give a second consequence**

Caregiver: *"I know this is difficult for you, John, but for not showing self-control, you have earned another consequence.* (This consequence is predetermined.) *You can earn some of these consequences back if you calm down and work with me right now."*

John: (yelling and pacing) *"Go to hell! I don't give a damn about your stupid consequences."*

Caregiver: (pause)

● **Provide a final opportunity for the youth to work through the original issue; give a positive correction statement**

Caregiver: *"John, you can begin making some good choices right now and begin working with me. Then you can earn back some of the consequences. Can you do that?"*

John: (yelling and pacing) *"Shut up and leave me alone, damn it!"*

Phase II – De-escalating Behavior

● Choose a self-control strategy

Caregiver: *"John, I know this is really tough for you and you are angry. But you do have some choices. Can you choose a self-control strategy?"*

John: *"You bet I'm pissed off! You're always out to get me!"*

Caregiver: *"Deep-breathing is one of your self-control strategies. Why don't you take some deep breaths like we practiced to calm yourself down."*

John: *"That crap is stupid! I'm not doing that."*

Use the four ongoing tools to help the youth regain self-control.

● Praise improvements in behavior

John: (stops pacing)

Caregiver: *"Great, John, you've stopped pacing. You're starting to make some good choices."*

John: (sits down and yells) *"I want to call my mom!"*

Caregiver: (pause)

● **Give a reality statement**

Caregiver: *"Great job of staying in the chair. Once we work through this issue, we can talk about calling your mom."*

John: (yelling) *"I have the right to call my mom. I want to call her now!"*

Caregiver: (pause)

● **Describe what was done wrong, and describe what to do right**

Caregiver: *"I understand you have some concerns. Right now you're yelling and a better choice is to stop talking and listen."*

John: (stops talking and remains sitting)

Caregiver: (pause)

● **Praise improvements in behavior**

Caregiver: *"You've stopped talking; nice job of following instructions, John. You are starting to show some self-control."*

John: (remains in seat, quiet and angrily looking away)

Caregiver: (pause)

● **Statement of understanding**

Caregiver: *"I know this is tough, John, and I know you're angry and upset."*

Note: Continue using the four tools until the youth engages in his or her self-control strategy and begins to calm down. Keep in mind that the length of the pauses will vary depending on the child's behavior. It is critical during this phase to provide the child with space so that he or she can stop the inappropriate behaviors. If a tool doesn't seem to be working or is causing the youth's behavior to escalate, stop using it and try another tool. Don't rush the process. Give ample time for the tools you are using to work.

John: (uses deep-breathing strategy and appears to calm down)

● **Test for self-control with simple instructions**

Caregiver: *"John, you've done a nice job of getting yourself under control. You've done your deep-breathing and you are remaining quiet and seated in the chair. I'm going to give you an instruction to check if you are ready to work through this problem."*

John: *"Okay."*

Caregiver: *"Thanks for using a pleasant voice tone. Great! I'm going to ask you to go pick up the chair you knocked over. Remember to look at me, say 'Okay,' pick up the chair, and say, 'Is there anything else?'"*

John: (responds appropriately to the instruction)

Caregiver: (specifically describes and praises appropriate behavior; practices one more instruction with the youth)

● **Review behaviors that demonstrate self-control**

Caregiver: *"You're doing a fantastic job of demonstrating self-control, John. Remember during the rest of the time to use a calm voice tone, look at me, sit up straight, and give me an answer. Okay?"*

John: (responds appropriately)

Phase III – Cognitive Strategies

(Keep in mind that the caregiver chose a self-control strategy for John.)

- **Prompt how to accept consequences (or practice)**

  Caregiver: *"John you've done a super job calming down. Keep it up. Do you remember how to accept consequences?"*

  John: (calmly) *"Yeah."*

- **Review the consequences the youth earned**

  Caregiver: *"You have earned a consequence for not choosing a self-control strategy and a consequence for originally not accepting 'No' for an answer. But, you can earn some of those consequences back when we practice."*

  John: *"Okay."*

  Caregiver: *"Great job of accepting those consequences!"*

- **Review and practice a self-control strategy**

  Caregiver: *"Okay, let's first look at what you can do the next time you get upset. Remember that when you want to use deep-breathing, or are asked to use it, you should take a deep breath in through your nose and hold it for about two seconds, let the breath out slowly through your mouth, repeat this until you feel yourself calming down, and when you are calm, tell an adult. Remember those steps?"*

John: *"Yeah. I just lost it."*

Caregiver: (asks John what other settings and situations he may be able to use this self-control strategy and why using a strategy is important)

Caregiver: *"Are you ready to practice this?"*

John: *"Okay."*

Caregiver: *"Remember: This is just a practice. I'm going to tell you that you can't watch TV. Remember what to do?"*

John: *"Yeah."* (calmly asks to sit on the couch and does deep-breathing)

Caregiver: *"Great! You asked me if you could go sit on the couch, and you practiced how to use deep-breathing to calm yourself down. And you asked me in a quiet voice. Nice! It's important to remember to use one of your strategies*

165

the next time you get upset, no matter where you are or whom you're with. Since you did such a good practice you have earned back half back of the first consequence."

John also earns a positive consequence for the behaviors he or she is currently using that demonstrate self-control.

Caregiver: *"John, right now you are using a calm voice, sitting down, and really working well with me on practicing these skills. You are demonstrating self-control and have earned a positive consequence."*

● Return to the original issue and begin a Corrective Teaching Interaction

Caregiver: *"Let's talk about the original issue of not accepting 'No' for an answer. In the future, when you are given a 'No' answer you should...."* (The caregiver would finish a Corrective Teaching Interaction and the child could earn up to half of the consequence back for an acceptable practice.)

Summary

One of the most significant treatment objectives of the Boys Town Teaching Model is teaching troubled kids various individual, effective, therapeutic strategies for maintaining self-control. These children and adolescents experience many unpleasant feelings (e.g., sadness, anger, jealously, and so on) due to traumatic events in their lives. These overwhelming feelings often are expressed in negative behaviors when a crisis occurs. Youth have learned to erupt in aggressive, violent, and self-destructive ways when confronted with these unstable feelings. In these situations, a process called Crisis Teaching is used to help youth regain self-control and learn self-control strategies. These strategies help troubled kids deal with these unpleasant feelings, anticipate crisis events, and calm themselves instead of exploding with combative, antagonistic, and damaging behaviors. In this way, youth learn different methods to successfully manage crisis situations and get their needs met in a more socially appropriate manner.

Reference

Long, N.J., & Wood, M.M. (1991). **Life space interaction.** Austin, TX: PRO-ED, Inc.

Reducing Aggression in Children

"The life of the nation is the life of the family written large."

– Plato

Over the years, many people have asked Boys Town staff, "How do I teach my child to be a considerate person, one who doesn't act aggressively toward others yet doesn't get pushed around?" For this reason, Boys Town would like to share strategies that have been effective in helping some aggressive children to learn and develop these social abilities. These procedures are fairly straightforward and can be used by psychiatric nurses, teachers, child-care workers, or parents. We hope you will find them beneficial. (For ease of reading, we often will use only the pronoun "his" or "him.")

169

How to Know
If a Child Is Too Aggressive

Although we all know what aggression is, here is the definition we prefer to use: "...directly standing up for one's personal rights and expressing thoughts, feelings and beliefs in a way that is often dishonest, usually inappropriate and always violates the rights of the other person" (Lange & Jakubowski, 1976).

Almost all children at one time or another get into a fight with their friends or siblings. In fact, studies show that 50 percent of the interactions between one-year-olds and two-year-olds can be viewed as "aggressive" (Cairns, 1979). While this may be of some concern to caregivers (because of its effect on the family), these behaviors are more of the "garden variety" type of aggressive acts. These children may have infrequent episodes of aggressive behavior in their lives, but it is not an ongoing problem for them. Learning a few skills will help most caregivers handle these problems as they arise.

There are other caregivers, however, who eventually begin to suspect that a child's repeated aggression is something more serious. These caregivers not only witness the child's aggressive behavior, but also hear about it from parents, babysitters, day-care workers, and teachers. Naturally, this is frightening to them. In some cases, these caregivers need not worry. But most of the time their concerns are appropriate.

To help caregivers determine if their concerns are valid, we provide the following list of cues that indicate that a child may continue to display aggressive behavior as an adult.

1. Displaying aggressive behavior at an early age. There is research that says that if no intervention occurs to change aggressive behavior, children who will become "career" antisocial adults can be identified as early as age six. Thus, the child who is constantly hitting his peers at age seven is going to be more difficult to change than the child who gets into his first fight at 14. Typically, children who engage in frequent and serious aggressive behavior prior to age 10 would fall into this category. This type of behavior has often been unintentionally reinforced early in the child's life. For example, a mother takes her three-year-old shopping at the grocery store. When they get to the checkout line, the child asks his mother for some candy. Mom says "No." The child begins to whine and beg for the candy. Mom says "No" again. The child then raises his voice and begins to scream and cry. The mother becomes embarrassed and tries to quiet the child. When this fails and the child continues to scream, the mother gives in and lets the child have the candy. The child is reinforced for screaming because he got what he wanted. The mother is reinforced because the child is now quiet. This pattern will be repeated often because both people got what they wanted.

2. Displaying many different types of aggressive behaviors, in a large number of situations, with many different people. This means that a child who gets into fights with peers, is often removed from the classroom for cursing his teacher, and threatens to hit his parents when they attempt to discipline him, is much more likely to engage in antisocial behavior as an adult than a child who occasionally gets into fights with peers.

3. The frequency of aggressive behavior. A large number of aggressive behaviors that occur independently of each other indicates continued aggression. This means it is going to be more difficult to help the child who loses his temper quickly and frequently than the child who loses his temper occasionally.

4. The seriousness of the behavior. The seriousness of the behavior can be determined by whether the child engages in behaviors that could cause the police or courts to become involved. Some examples would be theft, vandalism, and violence toward another person. A child who engages in these types of behaviors is likely to continue these behaviors as an adult. When determining the severity of a child's behavior, there are four levels of intensity to consider. The least serious level would be when a child is noncompliant and won't do what is asked. The next level would be when a child gets angry or upset and makes verbal threats. The third level would be when a child destroys property. (This can range from tearing up a piece of paper to punching holes in the wall, or throwing dishes or furniture.) The last, and most serious level, is when a child actually becomes physically aggressive toward other people (peers, parents, teachers, etc.)

5. The length of time that the child is out of control. Some children lose control of their behavior quickly and regain it quickly. Others get upset quickly and lose control of their behavior for hours. They also reject any attempts at helping them calm down. The child who is able to calm down quickly is less likely to be involved in a serious situation, while the child who takes longer to cool down is more likely to engage in a variety of inappropriate, aggressive behaviors.

These cues will help the majority of care-givers understand that a child's aggressive activity falls into the "garden variety" category. This should alleviate some fear. At the same time, the techniques described in this paper can be used to help diminish any aggressive tendencies the child does have.

Adult Skill in Reducing Childhood Aggression

In dealing with children who come to Boys Town with serious aggression problems, we have found it effective to measure the frequency, length, and severity of out-of-control episodes that occur with these children. Most professionals do not monitor or measure these three factors, making it difficult for them to determine whether or not a child is making progress. This may lead adults to become reactive teachers, rather than proactive teachers. Staff at Boys Town use a proactive approach by teaching kids to monitor their own behavior after they lose self-control. This often helps a child take ownership of his or her behavior and is helpful in reducing the aggression. If you have a child who is displaying behaviors that are more serious than those described earlier as "garden variety," we strongly recommend that you have the child chart the number of times he or she loses self-control, the severity of the incidents, and the length of the episode. Often, just making the child more aware of the behavior by having him or her mark a chart will decrease the aggression to some extent.

To change any aggressive behavior, care-givers might find it helpful to view aggression as an interactive event. In these situations, adults must teach children how to replace their current aggressive behaviors with more socially appropriate behaviors that do not cause the child to be abusive toward others. It should be noted here that a child often teaches an adult to behave inappropriately faster than an adult can teach a child to behave appropriately. For example, consider a child who loses control of his behavior, refuses to follow instructions, screams, runs around, makes negative statements, cusses, makes threats, and damages property. All these behaviors can cause an adult to feel frustration, anger, and even fear. At this point, the adult has two choices: 1) "get even" with the child by showing him who is in charge (punish), or, 2) teach the child. It would be understandable if the adult responded by getting even: raising his voice, giving commands, and losing self-control. If this happens, the child, in a sense, is teaching the adult to behave inappropriately at a faster rate than the adult is teaching the child to behave appropriately.

The adult's intent might be to get even by punishing the child, but this only serves to reinforce the child, which can cause him to escalate his behaviors. Given this scenario, the adult needs to ask himself, "Do I want to get even and show this kid who is in charge, or do I want to teach?" Although it probably will be more difficult to decide to teach, you will find that teaching will be much more helpful in the long run.

Sometimes when a child is angry and engaging in aggressive behavior, it is easy to feel that the child is acting that way intentionally and is even enjoying it. This happens more often with children who initiate aggressive behaviors. But for kids who don't initiate the aggressive interactions, you commonly will find that these types of behaviors are as painful for the child as they are for the adult who is trying to help. That's why it is important, regardless of how inappropriate the child's behavior might be, that you don't treat the child with disrespect. (Kids call this "dissing.") With this in mind, here are some steps that can be used to show respect for a child as you help him or her calm down and teach some alternative behaviors. These steps can be effective with children who initiate aggression and children who respond aggressively to provocation.

1. Stay calm. The most important thing to do is stay calm. No matter how aggressive or angry the child is, you have to remain calm and in control of your own behavior if you are going to help him.

2. Use request statements. When interacting with a child, it is necessary to give instructions to change his or her behavior. Instead of trying to coerce the child into changing by making demands or threats, you should make requests. Let's take an example where you ask a child to make his bed. After a while, you notice that the bed has not been made. A person who wants to "control" the child would say something like, "Make your bed right now or you're grounded" in a loud and demanding voice. But rather than getting the child to make his bed, this response angers the child and accelerates his inappropriate behavior. Remember, your role is not to control or force the child. You have control and force by the very fact that you are an adult. Don't be an aggressive adult – that won't help the child in the long run. Instead, be an empathic adult who helps the child understand what he needs to do to get his own behavior under control. Using words such as "Please" and "Thank you" lets the child know that you are there to help, and makes it more likely that he will respond to your requests.

Examples include, "Would you please lower your voice?" or "Would you please sit down?"

3. Describe appropriate behavior. Often, a child engages in aggressive behavior because he has forgotten, or never learned, how to react appropriately in particular situations. The first key to describing appropriate behavior is being specific. Statements such as, "Be good," are too vague for the child to understand – they don't adequately explain what type of behavior is expected. By specifically describing how you want the child to change a behavior, you are setting him up for success. When you clearly and specifically state what you would like the child to do, he is more likely to try to get his needs met without getting angry! Thus, saying things like, "Could you please lower your voice?" or "I would appreciate it if you could sit down on the couch and talk with me," are much clearer, and help the child understand exactly what is expected.

4. Avoid nagging. When dealing with children who are acting aggressively, our tendency often is to go on and on about what they are doing wrong. Comments such as, "You're always getting mad, screaming and yelling and causing problems," or "Every time I try to talk with you, you get angry and stomp and scream and you never do what I ask," make the child feel like you are "hassling" or "nagging" him. This is coercive behavior, not unlike that of the proactive aggressive child. It not only tends to escalate the child's aggressive behavior, but also makes it hard for you to like yourself. It also is poor role-modeling for the child. To avoid nagging, keep your descriptions of the child's inappropriate behavior brief and objective. If you feel that the child is so used to hearing you say what is wrong that he won't listen, try ignoring the inappropriate behavior. If the behavior can't be ignored, saying things like, "You're shouting" or "You're raising your fist," can help you to avoid making negative statements about the child and get your point across without belaboring the issue. Whatever you do, try to resist the urge to describe everything the child has ever done wrong, and focus instead on what you would like to see him change.

5. Express concern and empathy. For many aggressive children, this may be the first time someone has worked through a problem with them. When one of these children engaged in aggressive behavior in the past, an adult probably just gave in and gave the child what he or she wanted, or "abandoned" the child by turning the problem over to someone else. (How often have

179

you heard an adult tell a child, "Do whatever you want. I don't care"?)

One way to let a child know that you are going to help him work through his behaviors in a positive manner, without giving in to his aggressive demands, is by using statements such as, "I know this is really hard for you," "I can understand that this is upsetting," or "I really want to help you." These types of comments are effective with both the child who initiates aggression and the one who responds to it, and helps to make the child less fearful that you will abandon him because of the behavior. They also remind the child that you are there because you are concerned and want to help.

One of the most important things to remember in these situations is that time is on your side! It may seem to take forever to stop the behavior the first few times you refuse to give in to a child and insist on working through the situation, but the child will quickly learn that you are going to stay with him. As a result, you will quickly see these interactions become shorter.

6. Focus on the positive. Even in the worst situations, you will find something that the child is doing right if you look hard enough. When a child is very angry, it often takes awhile for him to calm down. This usually happens gradually as the child's behaviors diminish one by one. If you can look for these gradual improvements, and reinforce a child for them as he calms down, it can help the child see that you are being fair in these situations and not just focusing on what he does wrong. Reinforcement can be something as simple as saying, "I know it's hard to lower your voice," or "Thanks for putting your fist down," but it can go a long way toward helping the child see that you are on his side.

7. Offer a cool-down time. Since the child is used to having adults give in to the aggressive behavior, he probably will become more angry, more coercive, or even more aggressive when you do not give in. If you think about a time when you were really angry, you might remember that it took awhile to cool down. You also might realize that if you had tried to deal with that situation at that particular moment, things might not have gone too well. The same is true for kids. Teach the child that if he can control his aggressive behavior, you will provide some cool-down time before he has to deal with the situation. How you do this will depend upon the child and situation. Remember, you are not trying to teach the child that it is wrong to get angry, only that it is wrong for a person to act aggressively when he is angry.

8. Teach an alternative behavior. Anytime a child behaves aggressively, you should teach the child alternative ways to meet his needs. We all have needs, but most of us have learned socially appropriate ways of getting these needs met. For example, if you go to your boss and scream and yell that you don't think you're getting paid enough, in all likelihood, you're not going to get a raise. You may even lose your job! On the other hand, if you go in and give your boss examples of jobs you have completed on time, and other ways you have been an asset to the company, and do so in a calm and respectful manner, the odds of getting that raise are greatly increased. The same is true for kids. If a child wants to join a baseball game, and he tells the other children he's going to beat them up if they don't let him play, those kids are not going to be too excited about letting him play. This child needs to learn how to approach other children, and how to ask permission to play with them.

When you are working with an aggressive child, it often is helpful to look at what happens just prior to the child's aggressive behavior. This can give you a clue about what skills the child needs to learn. For instance, Aaron comes in and politely asks if he can go to the store. When you tell him "No," he begins to scream and swear. The behavior that occurred just before Aaron started screaming and swearing was you giving him a "No" answer. This should tell you that Aaron needs help learning how to stay calm when he is told "No." You could break this skill into steps for him: "Whenever someone in authority tells you 'No,' you need to look at the person; say 'All right, I understand' or something similar; and, if you have a question about the 'No' answer, ask it in a calm, pleasant voice tone."

A few of the more common skills that aggressive children have difficulties with include: accepting "No" answers, accepting criticism, responding to teasing, asking permission, asking for help, and accepting consequences. Breaking these skills into steps, and teaching the child how to respond appropriately to these situations, provides the child with alternatives to aggression.

9. Work one-on-one with the child. A child may feel somewhat intimidated by an adult, both because the adult often appears to have more power than the child and because the adult is often bigger than the child. A child may feel even more overwhelmed when two or more adults are involved in a situation. If you are concerned that a child may become physically aggressive, you should have another adult nearby who can hear what is going on and can help if necessary. But only one adult at a time should work with the child, and if at all possible, it should be the adult who was with the child when the problem began. Otherwise, the conflict between the child and that adult may not be resolved. If an interaction is particularly long, it's okay for someone to take over so that the first adult can take a break, as long as the first adult returns to finish the interaction.

10. Monitor your own behavior. When you see someone engaging in aggressive behavior, the typical urge is to escalate your own behavior to match that of the other person's, especially if the aggression is directed at you. The other person then escalates his or her behavior, causing you to get angrier. It goes back and forth until both people are out of control. That's why it is so important for you to remember, when a child is screaming and yelling at you and you can feel your anger rising, that you are a role model for the child. It's going to be very difficult to convince the child to control his aggressive behavior if he sees you engaging in the same behavior. If you are going to help children calm their aggressive behaviors, you have to be able to control your own behavior first. One way to do this is by trying not to speak too fast or too loudly. Typically, when a person gets upset, one of the first things he or she does is start talking faster and more loudly. If you talk softly and slowly, it is less likely that you will get upset. You also will find that if the child's voice is raised and you keep yours softer than normal, the child will eventually lower his voice to hear what you are saying.

Another thing to be aware of is your body posture. Make sure that you are relaxed and that your posture isn't signaling physical aggression or a possible confrontation. Be aware of your hand movements. Moving your hands too quickly, or pointing or wagging your finger at a child can be perceived as aggressive acts and may cause the child to respond with physical aggression. This is particularly true of children who have been physically abused; they may think you are going to hurt them and they may lash out to protect themselves. For this reason, it also is important that you give the child enough space so that he won't feel crowded or backed into a corner. A good rule of thumb is to stay at least an arm's length away from the child. This gives most people a fair amount of "private" space, and helps to protect you from being hurt if the child does lash out. Remember also that your goal is to calm the situation. If your face is showing anger (lips tight, teeth clenched, glaring), the child will feel that you are angry and upset with him, and he will be less likely to calm down.

Teaching the Aggressive Child to See the World Differently

Often, a child's aggressive tendencies are increased because of distorted thinking. Cognitive distortions undermine the child's ability to perceive what others are experiencing and to read the cues that others are providing. Typically, there are four common cognitive distortions that aggressive children engage in. They are:

1. Arbitrary inference – misperceiving a social cue or "mind-reading" another's intentions; in other words, drawing a conclusion from insufficient or contradictory information. An example would be a situation where Bob is struggling with a math paper when one of the "smarter" kids comes over and offers to help. Although the offer is genuine, Bob perceives that the youth is asking to help only so that he can make fun of Bob in front of the other kids. So Bob tells the youth to "shove it," and swings at him with his arm. Another example might be a situation in which Margaret has moved and is going to attend a new school. Before she even gets to school, her thinking is distorted because she already believes that the new kids won't like her and will be "out to get her." Her first day on the playground, Margaret sees another little girl walking toward her; she runs over and knocks the girl down.

186

2. Magnification – exaggerating the meaning of an event, or catastrophizing ("making a mountain out of a molehill"). An example would be a situation in which Patty is caught cheating on a test. Although she's disappointed at getting caught, she does not feel it's fair that she receives a detention. She begins to rant and rave, yelling, "I've never had a detention. You're ruining my whole life. I won't even be able to go out this weekend." She then begins to swear and tells the teacher that she better "back off."

3. Dichotomous reasoning – overly simplified and rigid perceptions of events as all or nothing, or always or never. For example, some fourth-grade boys are choosing sides for football at recess. John wants to be his team's quarterback, but the other kids decide to let Bill do it. John gets angry and yells, "You never let me do anything!" He then starts hitting and kicking the other kids.

4. Overgeneralization – taking a single incident, such as failure, as a sign of total incompetence. Consider this example: Karen, a sixth-grader, is watching the other girls play volleyball at recess. They ask her to join them, but she says she can't play. They tell her she just needs to try it, so she joins the game. When the ball is served to her, she hits it too hard and it goes out of bounds. She gets angry and says, "I told you I can't play!" Then she shoves two girls out of her way as she stomps off the court.

Children who engage in distorted thinking will need many helpful conversations with a concerned adult. They will need much encouragement to change not only their behavior, but also how they see the world. Remember, their world view is part of the problem. When a child stomps off the football field or blows up in the classroom, someone will need to talk with him, not just to calm him down, but to help him see a different side of the situation. Having these children make apologies is another crucial part of this process; an apology is their verbal acknowledgment that their view of the circumstances was wrong.

As you talk with these children, you can help them restructure their distortions. Here are some simple steps you can teach that can help a child learn how to do this:

1. Recognize physical responses to anger. At a neutral time, try to help the child identify what physical symptom appears when he first begins to feel anger. Some possible symptoms are sweaty palms, clenched teeth, stiffening of the shoulders, face feeling flushed, etc. The child may have a difficult time defining a particular symptom, and you may need to watch closely the next few times the child gets angry to see if you can help identify it. Once the child is aware of this first physical symptom of anger, he can go on to the following steps.

2. Stop and make a self-calming statement. Help the child to understand that as soon as he experiences that first physical symptom of anger, he should tell himself to stop and make a self-calming statement. Examples of such statements include, "It's going to be okay; just take a second to calm down"; "This may not be as bad as I think. Let me calm down for a second"; or "Okay, just count to 10 and stay calm."

3. Evaluate the thoughts. Help the child to see that he sometimes has a thought that is not accurate before he becomes aggressive. Try to talk the child through recent aggressive situations to help him identify what that initial thought may have been. Once the child understands how this happens, he can learn how to make the self-calming statement, and then try to figure out what thought occurred before he began to feel anger. Teach the child to identify the distortion. Examples of such thoughts include, "She just hates me," or "It's his fault I missed the ball." Also, many of us have basic, common "put-downs" for ourselves that are distorted. So the child could be thinking something like, "I never do anything right," or "I'm just stupid." Once the distortion is identified, teach the child to make a self-statement to address the distortion. Examples of such statements include, "Maybe she doesn't really hate me. She might be trying to help me"; "It might not be his fault I missed the ball. He may have overthrown it by accident"; or "I'm not dumb. I just make mistakes like everyone else."

4. Think about options, and choose one. Teach the child to take a few minutes to think about his options before reacting. Remind the child about the consequences of choosing to become aggressive, and tell him to think about all the alternative ways he could react in this situation. Teach the child to choose a positive alternative from the options and try it. Emphasize that he will not know if alternatives will work unless he is willing to give them a try. Explain that other alternatives often can have pleasant results, and that if the child is willing to take a risk, he will experience some of these over time.

5. Develop a self-corrective process. Help the child learn how to document situations that occur and how to share them with you. Ask questions and help the child explore whether or not he was able to change the distorted thinking and if he feels comfortable with the outcome. It is extremely important that you praise and reinforce the child for any effort to change his thinking, even if he doesn't select the best choice possible. Remember, all change takes time. Do not expect success immediately or consistently.

6. Look at the other person's perspective. While the child is thinking about past situations, have him document the perspective of other people who were involved. Tell him to write down what he thought the other person was thinking and feeling. Getting aggressive children to see other people's perspectives is important. If they distort the other person's point of view, help them to see how things really were. If a child can develop empathy for others, he is far less likely to engage in abusive behavior.

7. Don't expect perfection. Remind the child that change is difficult for everyone. Tell him that it would be great if he could start out by remembering one or two of these steps. Let the child know that he eventually will be able to do all of these steps, but not to expect that to occur immediately. Encourage the child not to lose heart if he doesn't do it exactly right the first time.

8. Set goals. The aggressive child needs realistic goals. If a child has been "blowing up" in the classroom twice a week, trying to reduce that to one "blowup" a week might be a reasonable goal to start with. Chart the frequency of the behavior and discuss progress with the child daily. Be sure to give lots of encouragement and praise.

The Effects of Relationships on Aggressive Children

A final way to help decrease a child's aggressive behavior is relationship development.

One of the most positive aspects of relationship-building is that it can be used to reinforce a child for controlling his own behavior. If a child feels close to you and likes you, he is more likely to want to please you. You can demonstrate your pleasure with the child's behavior by providing social rewards. For example, one of the best things you can do when a child has successfully controlled his behavior is to give him a hug. Remember, however, that hugging is appropriate only if you have a strong relationship with the child, and the child is willing to receive the hug and give you one back. Clear boundaries also must be set so that this demonstration of your happiness with the child is not misinterpreted as anything other than a maternal or paternal hug.

Another area of relationship development that can be beneficial to the aggressive child is the ability to communicate respect for others. Since aggressive children often get their needs met at the expense of others, it is important to help them become aware of the feelings and rights of others. It can be helpful to let a child know what you are feeling in situations where he does not respect your rights. It also is important to help the child recognize how he feels when others hurt his feelings. You may have to help him identify these feelings. Using an emotions chart and helping the child to pick out the emotion he is feeling can be very beneficial.

Humor is one of the more reinforcing aspects of a relationship. Aggressive children often have difficulty with this, however, because they don't know what appropriate humor is and when it can be used. It is not unusual for the aggressive child to be the "class clown" who often uses humor when others are trying to work or hold serious discussions. Often, these children have difficulty understanding the differences between inappropriate and appropriate humor. They may publicly tease others about sensitive issues or use humor at the expense of others. These kids, though quick to tease others, have a very difficult time laughing at themselves. Teaching these children to use humor effectively can help enhance their relationships with others. This can be done by reinforcing them when they use appropriate humor and ignoring them or providing consequences when they use inappropriate humor. Using praise and positive consequences can be very effective in helping these children learn that it is okay to laugh at themselves. One of the strongest ways to teach this is by role-modeling the use of appropriate humor and allowing the child to tease you so you can appropriately laugh at yourself.

Summary

Working with aggressive children can be difficult and frustrating. But remember that time is on your side. This article provides a foundation for helping children curb their aggressive behaviors. If you follow these steps, and are patient and concerned about the child, the rewards you receive as the child begins to learn to control his or her behavior will make all your efforts worthwhile.

References

Lange, A.J., & Jakubowski, P. (1976). **Responsible assertive behavior: Cognitive/behavioral procedures for trainers.** Champaign, IL: Research Press.

Cairns, R.B. (1979). **Social development: The origins and plasticity of interchanges.** San Francisco: W.H. Freeman.

Index

A

B

behaviors, 54-55, 63-64, 160-163, 171-173
   aggressive, cues, 171-173
   appropriate, 69, 75, 78
   arguing, 113-115, 138
   charting, 174
   de-escalating, 104, 130, 133, 160-163
   focus on, 110-112
   inappropriate, 68, 75, 78, 94
   monitor your own, 184-185
   negative, 66, 88, 90-92, 97, 99
   ongoing, 124
   positive, 65-66, 119
   responsibility for, 54
   review of, 163
   severity of, 145
   teach alternative, 182-183
body language, 38, 185
Boys Town, 5, 8-12, 15, 48, 56, 59, 63, 67, 71, 84, 88, 101, 148, 169, 174
Boys Town Teaching Model, 5-15, 59, 88, 102, 103, 150, 152, 154

C

Cairns, R.B., 170, 195
caregivers, 18-49, 87
   vital signs of relationships, 18-49
carpenter, example, 72
child, 80, 120-123
   age of, 80, 121, 144

N

O

P

W
walking in another person's shoes, 33
warmth, 70
Wood, M.M., 96, 98-99, 167

Z
Zits, 26